Highland Deer Stalking

Highland
Deer Stalking

David Hudson

The Crowood Press

First published in 1989 by
The Crowood Press
Ramsbury, Marlborough
Wiltshire SN8 2HE

British Library Cataloguing in Publication Data

Hudson, David
Highland deer stalking.
1. Great Britain. Deer. Stalking, Manuals
I. Title
799.2′597357

ISBN 1-85223-193-9

Photographs by David Hudson

Typeset by Photosetting, 6 Foundry House, Stars Lane, Yeovil, Somerset.
Printed in Great Britain by The Bath Press

Contents

Foreword

The red deer, the red grouse and the salmon are the three major sporting assets of Scotland's wildlife, and between them they attract many thousands of sportsmen to the Highlands every year. The red deer is not itself unique to Scotland, or even to Great Britain, as is the red grouse, but the techniques employed in the stalking of Scottish red deer are in many ways unique to Scotland. In the Scottish Highlands, the majority of red deer live out their lives on the open hill, and the so-called deer 'forests' are almost totally devoid of trees. Highland red deer stalking, therefore, is possible throughout the hours of daylight, unlike almost anywhere else in the world, where the deer are true forest animals, only emerging from the trees, to feed in the open, during the night. Stalking outside Scotland is usually confined to dawn and dusk forays. Virtually only in Scotland can stalking be considered as a daylight sport; and what more marvellous scenery than the Highlands can be imagined in which to enjoy it?

There have been many books written about the enchantment of stalking stags – the Monarchs of the High Tops or the Glens, as they are often called – and many also which describe the thrills of the pursuit of mighty stags or Muckle Harts. Many of these books have been wonderfully illustrated with evocative paintings of the Highland scene by famous artists both of yesterday and today. Most are wonderful reading and convey vividly the glories of Highland stalking. It is indeed a glorious sport – a sport which takes one into wonderful scenery, a physically demanding sport which requires skill, patience and expertise to achieve success, a solitary sport in many ways yet which can be closely shared with one or two companions. Though the goal is to kill deer, it is not a bloodthirsty sport (the actual killing of the beast is probably the least enjoyable part of the whole day in the eyes of most stalkers), but if one is to kill, one should know how to kill humanely, and having killed, not waste or squander any part of that kill. A successful shot is the culmination of the thrills and excitement of the stalk, but there still remains much hard work to be done in bringing the carcase home.

In this book, David Hudson sets out to describe the practical stalking scene for the last quarter of the twentieth century; he is not trying to emulate those wonderful books of the last century or the start of this century. He is trying to convey a modern scene on his canvas, highlighting the details which every stalker will want to know before he takes to the hills. He has done this, not with brush and pigment, but using his skills with camera and film, and has captured important moments throughout the whole year to convey what modern deer stalking is all about – the proper management of the largest wild animal of the

British mainland. He has set these scenes in perspective against a historical background of the animal itself and of the sport of Scottish stalking.

David is in an almost unique position to see the whole picture, living and working, as he does, in one of the larger and remoter deer forests of the Highlands. He sees the deer throughout the year. He sees and appreciates the incredible skill and devotion to duty of professional stalkers, not only during the stag stalking season, but also in their work throughout the year in managing and maintaining a healthy and productive herd of wild deer. He appreciates too, at first hand, the work required to maintain the infrastructure of a deer forest: the lodge, roads, pony paths, vehicles and often, boats. He can talk to the Rifles who come to enjoy the sport – some highly experienced with hundreds of stags to their credit, and others who have yet to see their first wild stag on the hill. He can discuss with both expert and beginner the merits or demerits of any particular piece of equipment, be it boots, breeches, balaclavas, binoculars or merely walking sticks; and he can hear their impressions of the day on the hill, which may or may not agree with what he hears from the stalkers.

David has produced a book with a wealth of useful, detailed information, which any inexperienced stalker will find invaluable, and from which many experienced ones will learn much. Not the least enjoyable part will be trying to produce the succulent dishes described in the chapter on Venison Cookery. Anyone fortunate enough to have sampled any of these dishes, prepared by David's charming wife, from across the Irish Sea, will know what I mean, and will surely agree.

Lord Joicey

Acknowledgements

Highland deer stalking is a wonderful field sport; not only because of the magnificence of the surroundings in which it is pursued, but also the pleasure of observing our largest wild animal – the red deer – in its natural habitat, totally un-confined by bars, walls or fences. The more I watch deer, the more I realise just how much there is to learn about them. In writing this book I have been fortunate to be able to call on the experience of a number of men who, in the course of their everyday work, spend many hours watching deer, and know more about the animals and their habits than I can ever hope to.

Albert Grant, Ronald MacDonald and Donny Mackay all helped with their great knowledge of deer, stalking and the Highlands, as well as accepting the presence of an extra 'stalker', complete with camera, on several trips to the hill. Lord Joicey, as well as kindly agreeing to write a foreword for this book, allowed me to accompany him and his guests on a number of stalking days. Chris Bennett helped with advice on the work of sporting agencies, Trevor Horsefield with the aims and objectives of the St Hubert Club of Great Britain and Hugh Oliver-Bellais with information on the British Deer Society. A number of people offered me photographic facilities in deer forests, including Lord Kimball, Martin Leslie and Derek Petrie, while Colin Taylor allowed me the run of his rod and gun shop for a day.

To them all, to Crawford Little who first suggested that I should write this book, and to my employers for their co-operation, my very sincere thanks.

David Hudson
Sutherland 1988

1

The Red Deer

In prehistoric times, Britain was roamed by many large mammals. Mammoth, bison, elk and reindeer wandered the primaeval forests and were preyed on by wolf, bear, lynx and sabre-toothed tiger. Successive ice ages drove the mammoth and sabre-toothed tiger into extinction, while the efforts of man later eliminated the wolf, bear and lynx. Bison and reindeer continued to thrive, though in other parts of the world, and by the sixteenth century most of the larger mammals, both prey species and predators, had gone from Britain.

Some vanished because of man. Bears and wolves were persecuted and hunted to extinction, the last wolf reputedly being killed around 1740 – some seven centuries after the last bear had vanished. It is interesting to speculate on the outcry that would arise now if the last survivors of one of our native mammals were about to be eliminated. A 'Save the Wolf' campaign would, no doubt, attract a great deal more support now than two hundred and fifty years ago, when bounties were still being paid for every wolf killed.

The loss of most of our larger predators was due to man making a conscious effort to eliminate those creatures he saw as a threat to himself and his domestic stock. Some other species declined, not because they were deliberately hunted to extinction, but because of the indirect effects of man on their environment. Vast tracts of forest were cut down for fuel and to clear land for agriculture, huge areas of low-lying marsh were drained and great stands of the native Highland forest were burnt as man sought to drive out wolves and, at times, other men. Many species failed to survive the relatively rapid changes in the British countryside which took place from Saxon times onwards. A notable exception, however, was the red deer.

Today, the red deer is our largest native mammal. While other species slid into decline, the red deer adapted to changes in the environment and climate and to the loss of much of its natural range, and is firmly established today – albeit somewhat changed from the animal which lived in our ancient forests. The red deer was certainly common in neolithic times and was already linked with man. Remnants of deer antlers have been excavated from Grimes Graves (ancient flint mines in the Norfolk brecklands). Miners used the antlers as picks and no doubt also utilised the meat and hides. There is evidence that in those days, deer were much larger than the animals to be found on the Scottish hills of the twentieth century – part of the price the species has had to pay for survival.

Although nowadays we associate the deer with the open hills and moors of the Highlands it is actually a forest animal, living by browsing as well as grazing. As man burnt and felled the woods that once covered most of Britain and claimed

11

A Highland red deer stag – our largest native wild animal.

the resulting farmlands for his own stock, so the deer were forced out on to ever more marginal land, eventually ranging principally over the bare, windswept hills of the north of Scotland. That they have managed to survive at all is remarkable, but survive they have. Indeed, they continue to do so in conditions that few other large mammals could tolerate. Compared to their natural, forest environment the hills are wetter, far colder and offer a level of feeding that is both mineral and nutrient deficient.

Fossil records indicate that the red deer reached its maximum size at the end of the last ice age, and that there has been a progressive decline in antler growth and body weight since that time. This decline has affected the red deer world wide, not just our British population. There has been a greater and much more rapid fall in the size of the Scottish red deer, however, and this is certainly due, not to any general trend among the species, but to the harsh conditions which the Highlands provide.

Evolved to live in the shelter of trees, the deer have nevertheless adapted superbly to life on the open hill. In winter, the Highlands can show a truly vicious face which would astonish those visitors who have admired the hills with their purple heather and brown bracken in late summer and autumn. The hills can assume a truly arctic aspect in the grip of a winter blizzard and life becomes a struggle to survive. The deer, lacking shelter and short of food, are forced to expend much of their energy maintaining bodily warmth. Since their diet is already considerably less rich than that of forest-dwelling beasts, it is little wonder that they never attain the same size and growth of antler that their low-ground cousins do. This is not a genetic change – Highland deer transported to a lowland environment are quite capable of matching the body size and antlers of animals which were bred there.

This small size may be a dual adaptation. We know that climate and food availability combine to restrict growth, but it may well be that, even if it were possible for a stag on the hill to reach the size of a woodland beast, there would not be enough nutrients available for him to maintain that bulk. In other words, hill stags, averaging seventeen stone live weight, may be at the optimum size for survival and breeding success. A lowland stag can reach double that weight and those from the continent perhaps three times as much. This is not to denigrate the red deer of the Scottish Highlands; they are magnificent animals in their own right.

The rigours of life on the open hill have affected the red deer in more ways than just the size they can attain. Hill stags cannot match the antler growth of low-ground stags, their antlers being smaller in all respects – length, circumference, weight and number of points. A hill hind reaches sexual maturity at a later age than her low-ground counterpart, and is likely to succeed in rearing a lesser number of calves in the course of her lifetime. Hill hinds are sexually mature at two or three years of age; the majority of woodland hinds reach sexual maturity as yearlings. Typically, Highland hinds will produce about forty-five calves per hundred, each year, compared with seventy calves per hundred of low-ground populations. Despite all their difficulties, the deer have been remarkably successful in adapting to their new environment. At the time of writing, it is estimated that there are 290,000 deer in Scotland – an increase on the estimated population of 180,000 for the 1960s – and this despite an annual cull of around 40,000 beasts.

For most of the year, stags and hinds lead separate lives, the stags occupying some areas in exclusively male groups (hence 'stag parties') while the hinds, calves and some of the younger stags live on other areas. It is only during the rut that the stags join the hind groups, and then only for a few weeks each autumn – the culmination of the year of the red deer, or perhaps the beginning since this is the time when new lives are started.

13

A hind with a calf and a follower in early October.

During the relatively easy days of summer, deer will be living on the higher ground, still in their separate groups according to sex. This is a time of comparative plenty, with a food supply that is more than sufficient to meet the animals' needs, though both sexes put extra strain on their resources at this time of year.

The hinds which mated successfully during the previous autumn will now have calves at foot and be putting much of their bodily effort into suckling them. Normally, only one calf is born to a red deer hind. Twins can occur and there have been one or two authenticated cases, but they are extremely rare. Hinds which have failed to conceive, or are calfless through still birth or miscarriage are known as yeld hinds. Often the calf of the previous year will stay with its mother even after the new calf is born, and the sight of a hind 'with a calf and a follower' is a familiar one to everyone who has stalked in the Highlands.

While the hinds are occupied with matters maternal, the stags too have a drain on their energies over and above the normal needs of survival. Each spring, they cast their antlers, then immediately begin to replace them by growing new ones. This annual replacement of several pounds of bony tissue must put an enormous strain on the stags' calcium reserves; and this at a time when they are at their lowest ebb, at the end of the winter. This is when most of the so-called 'winter mortality' actually occurs. By the end of the summer, however, antler growth will be complete. The soft covering of velvet which supplied nourishment to the

14

growing antler through its network of blood vessels will have been shed and the body weight of the stags will be at its maximum. The time of the rut approaches.

Towards the end of September, the stags begin to show signs of restlessness in their all-male groups. Their necks swell up to give them the characteristic maned look of a rutting stag and they begin to drift away, in ones and twos, from their normal summering grounds, wandering off in search of hinds. Sometimes they break out singly, but more often two stags are seen together – commonly a mature beast accompanied by a younger one – marching purposefully across the hill towards their chosen rutting ground.

The choice of an area in which to seek hinds may be something which a stag remembers from one year to the next. Their wandering off may, at times, be literally a search for hinds, but in many stags it is a ritual, repeated annually throughout their lives. A mature stag may have a particular area in which he gathers his harem of hinds each year, and he will go directly to that area when he breaks out, returning to his wintering ground at the end of his rut. At least, he will do this as long as he is strong enough to withstand the challenge from other stags. As, with old age, his strength and vigour are no longer sufficient to support his bid for supremacy, so he may have to wander further afield, leaving his normal ground in the possession of some fitter and heavier animal.

A stag during the rut can be an awesome sight. He will look relatively larger alongside the smaller hinds than when seen in the company of other stags, and the swelling of the muscles in his neck will add to this illusion of size. His blood heated by the call of the rut, he will eat practically nothing for the space of two or three weeks and rest only fitfully in that time. His whole world is governed by the need to collect a harem of hinds, to hold them despite the attentions of all other stags and to mate with each one as she comes into season.

A hind comes into season during the autumn, possibly triggered by day length, and if not mated during her season – which lasts about one day – will come into season again at approximately eighteen day intervals until a successful mating occurs. An oestrous hind will positively welcome the attentions of the stag, even going so far, at times, as to chivvy him to gain his attention, but the stag seems to hold little interest for the bulk of hinds being held by him. He may attempt to herd them, almost like a sheep-dog, and as often as not they will placidly ignore all his efforts and quietly get on with grazing, resting, or cud chewing. They seem to show no particular interest in the battles which are fought for their favours. It is not uncommon to see two evenly matched stags tussling for a bunch of hinds, so engrossed in their struggle that a smaller stag, who would never have considered challenging either contestant, nips in to drive some or all of the 'prize' away.

At this time of year the hinds will still be sporting the red coats of summer which give the species its name, but the stags will present a somewhat different aspect. Deer will wallow in peaty hags at any time of the year – to cool themselves, or to relieve the itch of some of the insects and parasites which can make the Highlands so trying for man and beast alike. At the time of the rut, stags are particularly prone to wallowing, using their feet and antlers to thrash the peat into a semi-liquid morass before sinking their whole body into it. They

15

Mid-winter and fresh snow dusts the ears and antlers of this old eleven pointer.

The same stag, photographed the following July. Rough-coated, and with very poor antlers, he was shot soon afterwards weighing only twelve stone.

emerge blackened and dripping like creatures from the imagination of a horror film maker. Before wallowing, they will often urinate into the wallow, coming out smelling almost as awesome as they look. The reasons for this behaviour are not certain. It may be to cool the heat of their blood, inflamed by the passions of the rut; it may be that, thus blackened, they present a larger and more fearsome sight to potential rivals, or, possibly, that this noisome, dripping creature (chunks of peat and vegetation clinging to his antlers), is in some way sexually attractive to the females. If the latter is the case, then it only works for female deer. A human male returning from a stalking day liberally coated with liquid, peaty slime is most unlikely to elicit thoughts of that nature from the woman in his life.

A stag will hold his hinds for two to three weeks, unless he is ousted by a larger, stronger rival during that time. If this happens, then he may wander off in search of other hinds, or he may join the other unsuccessful males hanging around the fringes of the hind groups, ever hopeful of picking up some of the crumbs from the master stags' tables. Once his passion is spent, the stag will leave the hinds and return to his wintering ground, thinner, possibly injured and certainly exhausted from his self-imposed regime of starvation and combat. This leaves the way open for some of the smaller, younger beasts to mate with those hinds which have been missed, or failed to conceive during the first few weeks of the rut.

Deer are not particularly vocal animals. Hinds may be heard bellowing during the calving season and will bark a warning when they perceive danger, a frightened calf will squeak for its mother and there is sometimes considerable quiet 'chatter' among groups of hinds and calves, but in general they make little noise that will reach human ears. During the rut, however, there is a complete change and from late September until December the hills and corries reverberate with the roars and counter-roars of rutting stags.

Heard from my bedroom window at night, as some lovesick brute bellows and moans among the rhododendrons for hour after hour, the roar of a stag is more annoying than impressive – like a cow with laryngitis, as my wife once described it. However, the full-throated roar of a master stag warning off a rival through the mists of an October morning is a completely different sound. Then, particularly if it is unexpected, it can be an awe inspiring noise, as indeed the stag intends it to be.

Red deer, in common with many species, have a well structured sequence of challenge and counter-challenge, threat and counter-threat, which takes place before any actual physical contest occurs. It is not in the overall interest of the species for the males to kill each other off during mating battles, and a pattern of behaviour has evolved whereby individuals can assess one another before combat is initiated.

Contact will often begin with a roar contest. A stag holding hinds roars to warn off potential rivals and in response to the roars of other stags. A stag with hinds is never at peace, even in the brief moments when he may lay down, a roar from anywhere in his vicinity will bring him leaping to his feet and trotting off in the direction of the threat. Sometimes, just the sound of a master stag may be

Deer are browsing as well as grazing animals, and can exhibit quite a degree of agility in search of a particularly tasty nibble.

enough to warn off a rival; at other times, the rival will advance closer and assess the opposition.

Most fights take place when two stags of approximately equal size dispute possession of a bunch of hinds. It is body weight that is important in deciding the result of these affairs; not antler size. It is not uncommon to see a hummel – a stag with no antlers – holding hinds, despite the attentions of apparently better armed adversaries. Where one stag has a considerable advantage in weight over his rival, the smaller stag will often retreat without offering battle – even if the smaller animal is actually holding hinds he may give them up without a fight.

If roaring and an initial sizing up of his opponent has not discouraged either stag then they will advance to within a few yards of each other. At this point a fight may occur immediately, or they may begin a parallel walk – striding up and down a few feet apart – the stag holding the hinds trying to keep his body between his rival and the harem. It is still possible that one or other may break off and run at this stage, chased away by the 'victor' without any actual fighting taking place. If not, then at any moment they may lock antlers and begin to battle in earnest.

Fighting usually takes the form of a pushing and twisting contest with locked antlers, each stag trying to force the other beast backwards. Being uphill bestows an obvious advantage on the higher contestant, and there is much twisting and turning, trying to gain the advantage of the higher ground. One stag will gain a purchase and drive his rival backwards for several yards, hooves

Early June. Antlers in velvet, coat soon to be cast and replaced with the sleek, red summer coat.

slithering and sliding through the peat, then, with a twist akin to a boxer escaping from a corner of the ring, the positions can be reversed, and the higher stag may find himself suddenly slipping backwards down the hill.

Occasionally a fight may last for several minutes. This is usually when the contestants are very evenly matched. More often, the action will last no more than a minute before one of the stags springs away and races off, hotly pursued by his erstwhile opponent for a hundred yards or so. Once the loser has been seen off in this fashion, the victor will return and round up his hinds again, unless some other stag has chivvied them away while his attentions were elsewhere. It is little wonder that stags look so exhausted when they finally drift back from their rutting activities, often with antler wounds or other injuries to heal before the onset of winter.

Winter, when it does come, can be long and hard. Snow cover can last from December to March and, at times, even into May, driving the beasts off the high tops and down into the slightly more hospitable glens and straths for shelter and access to grazing. Unfortunately, much of the forestry planting that has taken place since the war has taken place on the traditional wintering grounds of the deer and mile upon mile of high wire fencing has denied them access. This winter feed is of paramount importance to the deer. When the high tops are locked under an impenetrable covering of snow and ice, low-ground grazing is vital if the deer are to survive.

Many estates provide winter feed to supplement what the deer are able to find naturally on the hill. Stags are far easier to accustom to this free source of nourishment than are hinds, the female of the species harbouring a greater

Four stags, looking very moth-eaten as they begin to lose their winter coats, cooling down in a loch on a warm summer's day.

21

A good hind, feeding from hay put out by the stalker during a spell of severe cold and snow.

distrust of man than seems to be the case with the males. Stags will come readily to a daily handout of pulp nuts, maize, turnips, hay or potatoes, but it is much harder to bring the hinds down to feed. It can be done, and when hinds do condescend to accept a bite of hay from a human benefactor, they are far better mannered about it than are the stags.

Hay for hinds can be scattered in a continuous line and they will happily feed, shoulder to shoulder, with only the minimum of jostling. Try the same thing with stags, and fights will break out all along the line as the quarrelsome males squabble over every bite. For them the food must be spread around in well separated heaps, and even then there will still be a certain amount of jealous bickering over who eats where.

The food handed out by the estate staff will not normally be sufficient to sustain the beasts through the worst months of winter. It is more in the nature of a bribe – a regular bite of high–energy food that keeps both stags and hinds on the ground and may prevent them from drifting on to farmland or crofts in search of food, a search that will, all too often, result in death.

Provided that there is not too large a stock of deer on the ground, and that they have not been denied access to their traditional wintering grounds by forestry fences or an influx of sheep, then the red deer is better equipped than any other native animal for life on the winter hills. They can dig through quite deep snow in order to reach vegetation, scooping the snow aside with an elegant, flicking motion of the foreleg. Deep drifting may bring the deer within reach of some of the lower branches of the woodland birches and pines and heavy snow or winter gales can break off branches or bring down whole trees for the deer to browse.

Their metabolism has adapted to compensate, in some part, for the lack of food on the winter hills. Deer farmers have found that, even if their deer are wintered in sheds and given as much high-energy food as they wish, they still do not gain any significant weight throughout the winter months. It is only when the days lengthen to herald the beginning of spring that the beasts begin to convert their food into additional body weight. Equally, they will maintain their weight throughout the winter on quite a low-energy diet. It is as though there is some sort of change in their metabolic rate to compensate for the inadequate diet available in the winter and early spring.

When spring does finally come it will bring death for the weakest of the deer. The so-called 'winter mortality' actually takes place in the first weeks of spring when the deer, brought to their weakest level by the cold and semi-starvation of winter, finally succumb before the new growth of spring can save them. A cold, wet spring in the Highlands may mean that there is no real growth of food plants until well into May – too late for beasts already at a low ebb. Late calves, the oldest beasts and stags weakened or perhaps wounded during the rut, may well die now; sad to see, but nature's way of ensuring that those individuals most capable of perpetuating the species are the ones to survive.

For those that do live to see the new growth of spring turn the hills from brown to green again, spring is a time of re-growth. The hinds are becoming

Hinds and calves running along the lochside in anticipation of winter feed.

heavy with calves, grazing busily to build themselves up in readiness for suckling the offspring soon to be born. Most of the calves will arrive between the end of May and the end of June, so the hinds must take full advantage of the brief period of better nourishment prior to the births. Also in spring, the stags will cast their antlers, then immediately begin to grow replacement sets.

The earliest, which are usually the biggest stags, will cast in late March or early April and their antlers will often be well advanced in growth by the time that the smallest and youngest stags cast in mid-May. Casting may well be a painful process for the stags. I have seen stags shaking their heads as if in considerable discomfort immediately after an antler has been cast, often with a steady trickle of blood running from the socket on the skull where the antler was growing. Sometimes both antlers drop together, sometimes one may be gone for several days before the second is cast, giving the owner a curious, lop-sided appearance.

New growth is extremely rapid. No sooner has the old antler gone than a dark, velvet-covered knob can be seen swelling up from the pedicles. This develops with a speed that is almost visible, the new antler being covered with a reddish or grey/brown skin which has the texture (and name) of velvet. The antlers must be very sensitive at this time as stags can be seen standing up on their hind legs and boxing with their forefeet instead of engaging in their usual squabbles of push and shove using antlers.

At this time, too, they seem to be particularly sensitive to the attentions of the various biting insects that can so plague man and beast alike. Midges, clegs and horse-flies all like to take advantage of the rich supply of blood vessels that run through the velvet. On still, hot days the stags seek solace on the high tops where there is usually a breeze to keep them at bay, or they stand belly-deep in lochs or rivers.

Growing new antlers must put a considerable strain on the calcium reserves of stags and they compensate for this, to some extent, by chewing up their old antlers. Hinds will chew cast antlers as well and it is rarely that a cast antler can be picked up on the hill after the end of July. Seeing how quickly a stag can chew up an antler provides a salutary lesson on the grinding power of their molars – evolved to cope with grass, heather and twigs, but capable of demolishing an entire antler in a day or so.

As the new antlers develop, the stalker can see which stags are improving their heads (a 'head' refers to the antlers, not the actual skull of the stag in this context), and which are going back. At times, and particularly when a severe winter, illness or injury sustained in the rut, has sapped a beast's vitality, this change in antler quality can be quite dramatic. One stag, which I saw regularly, cast his eleven-point set of antlers and replaced them with a single spike on one side and two points on the other. This was caused by injury or illness rather than just old age. He was shot once the stalking season began and proved to weigh only twelve stone; this from an animal that would probably have made sixteen stone (larder weight) had he been killed the previous autumn. He certainly would not have survived the next winter – a clear case where swift death from a bullet was preferable to a lingering end from starvation.

A newly born calf, almost invisible in its dappled coat as it lies flat among the heather and deer grass.

By June, when the weather is normally warmer and the stags' antlers are becoming well developed, the hinds are busy with matters maternal. The bulk of calves are born in June, though the earliest will appear in late May and there may be births as late in the year as October (though a calf born at this time has much less of a chance of surviving through to the following spring). A newly born calf is a beautiful creature – huge, liquid eyes, velvety nostrils and a dappled coat which helps to camouflage it through the first, and most vulnerable, weeks of its life. There are no longer any predators in Britain capable of killing an adult red deer, but during the first few days of their lives, calves can be, and are, taken by both fox and eagle.

The maternal instinct is very strong in a hind and if she is close at hand then a mature hind is quite capable of fending off the attentions of either predator. However, in the first few days of life, the calf's defence is to lie still, trusting in the efficacy of its camouflaged coat to allow it to escape detection. Still too weak to follow the mother, the calf will lie, flattened to the ground among the heather, and wait patiently until she returns with nourishment.

Human disturbance may well be a contributory factor in the death of some calves at this age. Hill walkers who inadvertently drive the hinds away from their calving areas can, quite innocently, leave the calves exposed to the unwelcome attentions of fox or eagle, though it is unlikely that losses from such causes could ever have any significant effect on deer numbers. Once the calves are strong enough to accompany their mothers (at about a week or so old), they are far less likely to fall victim to a predator.

25

If undisturbed, the hind will normally stay in the vicinity of her offspring, acting particularly vigilantly at this time. A new-born calf will weigh from twelve to fifteen pounds, probably averaging fourteen pounds, and weight gain after birth is very rapid – about a pound a day. The calves quickly lose their dappled appearance and by the beginning of September most will be growing their winter coats. They are, perhaps, at their most attractive when seen in July and August – still in their dappled birth coats, dainty and playful as young lambs – in marked contrast to the more serious mien of their mothers. The mid-summer months should be carefree times for deer, with ample grazing, long hours of daylight and a warm sun on their backs, but there are problems even in this short time of plenty.

Flies and midges can conspire to drive the deer out on to the high tops throughout the summer months, especially if there are long hours of sunshine in July, when the clegs can drive both man and beast demented. Sunny days bring out the cleg, but if it is still and moist the midge – the curse of the Highlands – will appear to take its place. These biting insects affect man and deer alike, but of more serious consequence to the deer are two other insects: the nasal bot fly and the warble.

Nasal bot flies deposit their larvae in the nostrils of the deer and their grubs grow within the membranes of the nose. In a severe infestation they can cause death by blocking up the nasal passage completely. The warble is an internal parasite which grows into white, maggot-like grubs about half an inch long. It 'hatches' by eating its way out through the skin of the deer's back, causing

Still very wobbly on its feet, this calf tottered a few steps, then clapped down into the heather and was at once invisible.

intense irritation. In very bad cases, particularly in a young beast, there may be literally hundreds of these repulsive creatures burrowing their way out through the skin. Deer can also be affected by liver fluke and lung worm, but overall they are remarkably free from parasitic problems. Hill sheep and cattle are subject to a number of tick-borne diseases, notably louping-ill, but deer seem to be largely immune to the effects of tick bites, though they may be heavily infested with them.

By the time that stalking begins again (usually in August), the bulk of the calves will be quite well grown, the clegs should have vanished for another season and before long the first frosts of autumn will have driven the midges away for another year. It is a time when the hill is bursting with new life as the young creatures of the year begin to learn and practise those skills which must guard them throughout the rest of their lives. Fox cubs and wild cat kittens will be learning to hunt, as will the eagle chick, now fledged and soaring over the hill in company with its parents. Grouse and ptarmigan chicks are fully grown and almost ready to assert their independence of the adult birds while, all over the hill, breeding birds will be preparing for migration to their wintering grounds. Many – perhaps most – of the young will never live to see another summer, but that is the way of things and for every predator there has to be a prey species. One creature must die in order that others may live.

For the red deer – stags resplendent in their newly cleaned antlers and hinds with rapidly maturing calves at foot – it is almost time for the rut to begin again and for the start of new lives. All their natural predators have gone, defeated by evolution or hunted to extinction by man. There remains just one predator to hold the herds in balance. It is, of course, the most deadly of all predators – man.

2
History and Development

Venison must have formed part of man's diet from the earliest of times. Wherever deer and man occupied the same range, archaeologists have unearthed the remains of deer among litter – bits of bone, fragments of antler and the like – and deer are represented in many primitive cave paintings. We cannot know for certain how early man managed to kill an animal that was so much faster than himself. Various methods have been suggested, including driving deer over cliffs, digging pitfalls, luring the deer into them and spearing them from ambush. It is this last method that strikes me as the most probable. Though deer might be driven over a cliff, they are such sure-footed animals that it would be a very difficult 'accident' to arrange, and the labour involved in excavating a large enough pit to trap deer would be considerable, not to forget the problem of disposing of the spoil and camouflaging the hole in the ground well enough that an unsuspecting beast might tumble, or be driven into it.

Creeping to within spear throwing distance would seem to be a far more likely and straightforward method and would suggest that our ancestors were once accomplished deer stalkers. It would take great skill and patience to approach to within killing distance, but it would certainly be possible and would mean that a single hunter, alone and unaided, could stalk and kill his quarry. Where a group of early men hunted together it would perhaps be more likely that they would split into two parties – one group driving the deer to where the other lay in ambush with their spears. No matter how it was done, there is no doubt that early man did take a toll of the deer herds – and we have continued to do so ever since.

Much more is known about the hunting methods of historic times. The kings and nobles of England had large areas set aside as royal hunting preserves, where deer were protected by the most Draconian of laws. The kings hunted from horseback, chasing the deer with hounds, then shooting them with bow and arrow or crossbow and bolt.

Much of the terrain in the Highlands of Scotland was unsuitable, to say the least, for the pursuit of deer on horseback. Steep, rocky faces, boggy, wet moorland interspersed with pools and lochans, and boulder-strewn slopes were hardly the places to try riding a horse at speed, even though the deer coped well enough. Consequently, a different form of hunting was evolved. The deer were driven by the Highlanders – sometimes several hundred men working in concert – into some form of trap. There may have been a quite elaborate system of walls, of wood or stone, according to what was available locally, radiating out from a central enclosure into which the deer were herded and then slaughtered. More

A stag in early May looking lopsided and a little sorry for himself with one antler cast and the second soon to follow.

One day after casting. The pedicle has already healed and is showing the first signs of new growth.

simply, they may just have been driven through a narrow pass where the hunters lay concealed and waiting.

At times, great numbers of deer would have been killed in this way. It must have taken a considerable feat of organisation to ensure that hundreds of men, spread out over thousands of acres of hill, with no means of communication, managed to synchronise their efforts and prevent the deer breaking back through their lines to freedom. Once enclosed the slaughter must have been frightful, the hunters employing whatever weapons came to hand – swords, axes, clubs, bows and spears – to beat and hack the terrified animals to death.

No doubt such organised hunts were looked on by the participants as sport, but they were also a necessary part of survival in the Highlands. It was only at the end of the eighteenth century that visitors from the south began to come to the Highlands, in any numbers, specifically to hunt the deer, shoot the grouse and fish for salmon and trout.

A trip to the Highlands must have been a very considerable undertaking for those early sportsmen. General Wade's military roads, constructed in the early part of the century, had greatly improved travel in much of the Highlands, but there was no established system of communications, there were no sporting hotels, no stalkers and no ghillies to show them where and how to shoot or fish. Equally, there seems to have been very little restriction placed by the holders of lands on where or when a man might hunt. Indeed, from their own accounts, some of the earliest sportsmen seem to have wandered freely through much of the country, shooting and fishing wherever their fancy took them. It is interesting to speculate what might happen nowadays to anyone foolish enough to try and emulate them.

Changes in land use which took place in the latter part of the eighteenth century were to have a profound effect on the red deer in Scotland. The great sheep marches were cleared and developed in the fifty years from 1780 onwards, and the deer population fell to probably its lowest level for centuries. As the landowners discovered that they could earn a far higher rent by letting their ground out as sheep farms than they could ever hope to get from the crofters who struggled to make a living from their tiny holdings, so a great tide of sheep flowed into the Highlands. Thousands of people were evicted from their crofts in the now notorious clearances. The sheep affected the deer directly and indirectly – they competed for the available grazing, and where they took over the ground, deer were no longer preserved. Their numbers fell accordingly.

At the beginning of the nineteenth century there were only half a dozen estates which were still primarily concerned with the well-being of deer rather than sheep. Deer still existed throughout the Highlands, but in nowhere near the numbers of former times. They might well have declined even further, but it was at about this time that the first of the English sportsmen began to make the long journey north and, more importantly, began to describe the delights of shooting, stalking and fishing in both words and pictures.

Nor for the first time, and certainly not for the last, it was, paradoxically, the hunters who were the prime movers in the preservation of their quarry. In the beginning, the rents which visiting sportsmen were charged were minuscule, but

Definite signs of growth now, with a velvet covered knob on each pedicle.

they served to point the way. The seemingly inexorable tide of wool and mutton was halted, then reversed. The market for sheep products was to fall dramatically. From their low point, at the turn of the century, the deer made a steady comeback. More and more sheep marches were re-afforested; the sheep were removed (or greatly reduced in numbers), the deer protected again and their numbers allowed to rise.

As more and more sportsmen began to head north every year, so communications were improved to meet demand. The railways forged their way ever further northwards and regular boat services were established from London to Edinburgh and points further north. Spending summer in the Highlands had already become popular when, in 1842, Queen Victoria and Prince Albert made their first trip to the far north, setting the ultimate seal of respectability on to the fashion. The Royal couple did not, as has been suggested at times, actually start the great move to the north. English sportsmen had been coming to the Highlands, in ever increasing numbers, since the beginning of the century. However, they did, undoubtedly, add to the impetus. As summering among the Scottish mountains became 'the thing to do', so more and more areas were developed for their sporting potential. Sporting rents, naturally, rose accordingly.

The combination of improved communications and current fashion must have had a considerable effect on the average level of competence of the sportsmen who came to stalk and shoot. At the beginning of the nineteenth century, only

Antlers beginning to branch, and the winter coat showing the first signs of casting.

33

Two good stags, with antler growth almost complete, squabbling over a place to graze.

the keenest of shots would have had the energy and enthusiasm to undertake the long and arduous trip north and then accept the lack of creature comforts which would have greeted them on arrival. It follows that such men would probably, though not certainly, have been among the more skilled, or at least more practised, shots. When steamship services and railways, serving comfortable lodges and hotels, opened up the Highlands to anyone with the time and money to indulge their fancy for the then current fashion for all things Scots, the general standards of skill and sportsmanship must have suffered.

The influx of southerners, though much criticised then (and now, in certain quarters), brought a great deal of money into the Scottish economy and created thousands of jobs. Lodges were built for the comfort of the incomers, roads, railways and bridges were constructed all over the Highlands and a network of businesses, small and large, sprang up to supply the needs of visitors. Food and clothing, fuel, transport, sporting goods, boats, horses, laundries and even taxidermists were required, as well as all the workers directly associated with deer forests. There were keepers, stalkers, ghillies and ponymen to assist directly with the shooting and fishing; agents and factors to manage the estates in the owner's stead; cooks and cleaners, butlers and maids and all manner of others employed. The sporting estates may have been criticised as the playgrounds of the rich, but they did, and still do, bring work, business and money into areas where there are all too few alternative sources of employment.

It was during the latter part of the nineteenth century that the foundations of

A Victorian shooting lodge.

Bheallach (a pass through the mountains) at the bottom of Loch Choire, where the Duke of Sutherland and King Alfonso of Spain took part in one of the last great deer drives.

the sport of stalking, as we know it today, were laid. The practice of driving deer to waiting guns continued until well into the present century – the Duke of Sutherland organised a deer drive at Loch Choire as part of the entertainment when he was host to King Alfonso of Spain in 1928 – but long before this, stalking had become the accepted method of killing deer. This meant creeping to within range and then shooting them with a rifle.

There were several reasons for this. Deer driving required a great many men and a good deal of organisation, and in any case presupposed that deer were present in sufficient numbers and in places from which they could be driven to the selected killing ground. The deer population recovered rapidly as the great sheep marches were disbanded, but it is clear from contemporary accounts that there were nowhere near the number of deer in the forests that there are today. Besides, even if a successful drive could have been organised, the forests were much smaller than the vast areas of land which had been under the control of a single owner in the previous century. If the deer were driven, it was quite likely that they might be driven right off the ground and into a neighbouring forest. Since the deer were no longer to be brought to the sportsmen, it followed that the sportsmen must go to the deer.

Early stalkers went to the hill accompanied by their deer hounds as well as their rifles. The original task of deer hounds had been to course the stag until they succeeded in baying it (forcing the animal to stop and turn to face them), when the hunter would come up and despatch the beast with knife, musket or arrow. Later, the order of things was to be reversed, the stalker attempting to kill his quarry with a rifle first, then using the hounds to bay it or pull it down if the beast was wounded.

The muzzle-loading muskets and early rifles which the sportsmen were using were not only less accurate, but also considerably less powerful than the modern rifle, so the use of hounds to follow up wounded beasts was a common occurrence. As the development of breech-loading rifles, faster-burning propellants and improvements in the manufacture of rifles made available more accurate and far more powerful weapons, so the incidence of wounded beasts, and therefore the need for deer hounds, diminished.

The Victorians had what today seems to be a very callous attitude towards the animals they hunted. Wounding stags, whether because of deficiencies in the rifle or the marksman, was common, and the books and journals written by sportsmen of the time are full of tales of stags struck by bullets but lost. Often there is no mention of any attempt to follow up a wounded beast in order to despatch it, and only rarely does one find any hint of remorse for a fine animal condemned to a lingering and painful death.

Before we presume to judge our forbears too harshly it must be remembered that they only reflected the attitudes of the society in which they lived. If the lives of the animals they hunted were held cheaply, so too were the lives of men, in an age when war was considered almost as a sport. Rare birds were shot and mounted in glass cases, egg collecting was a respectable hobby, much in vogue with the clergy, and the Victorian naturalist would have carried a gun as naturally as his modern counterpart goes armed with camera and notebook.

Stalker and Rifle walking out to the hill – one of the things that has altered little since the last century.

Nevertheless, it was the Victorians who began to stalk for sport and in many ways the sport that they enjoyed then is identical to the sport we enjoy today.

Then, as now, the first task of the stalker was to get out to the hills where the deer were to be found. It was sometimes possible for the Victorian gentleman to ride out at least part of the way to the hill on ponyback, and today many stalkers will ride in some form of all-terrain vehicle for the start of their journey, but sooner or later, now as a century ago, the stalker will have to progress on his own two feet.

The Victorian stalkers prided themselves on the distances they could walk in the course of a day. The tenant of Badenloch, Charles Ackroyd, once spent an entire season living at the inn at Achentoul and walking eight miles, morning and evening, to reach and return from his shooting and stalking ground. That is, sixteen miles every day, in addition to the distance covered when shooting over pointers and stalking. How many of today's sportsmen would countenance that much exercise? In those days before the motor car, men and women were no doubt more accustomed to using their legs to get around, but the hills of the Highlands must still have been a severe test for many a southerner, especially those raised in the flat fields of East Anglia and the Home Counties.

The first of the touring sportsmen conducted much of their affairs on the hill, being accompanied by a man whose job it was to lead their hounds and carry their food and spare equipment. Later on, as more and more would-be stalkers

A stable where a ponyman would have lived during the season. This one is six miles from the shooting lodge and eighteen miles from the nearest public road.

flocked to the Highlands, there rose a demand for professional stalkers – men, skilled in the ways of deer, who could lead their gentlemen to where deer could be found, conduct the stalk to within range without alerting the beasts, instruct the sportsmen as to which animal to shoot, then gralloch, and arrange transport off the hill for the carcase.

Such was the success of this system that it has continued, little changed, right to the present day. Almost every forest now has its own staff of professional stalkers, and only the most experienced of sportsmen would ever be allowed to go to the hill to shoot a beast without a professional in attendance. Indeed, on many forests, the word of the head stalker is law. Everyone, including the owner of the forest who employs him, defers to his advice on all matters relating to shooting and stalking over the property.

In other ways, particularly with regard to the selection of which beasts are shot, a great deal has changed. The early stalkers were interested in trophy hunting. They wanted to shoot the biggest stags with the best heads and many a noble set of antlers adorns the walls of the shooting lodges, their erstwhile owner staring glassily out from beneath them. Despite this desire to shoot the best stags, in some ways the Victorians were not too particular what they shot, hinds and calves also falling victim to their rifles when nothing more suitable was easily available. While staying at Blair Castle as the guest of Lord and Lady Glenlyon, even Prince Albert shot two half-tame stags from one of the castle windows – hardly deer stalking, even by the most liberal definition.

Ackroyd describes a similar incident in his autobiography, *A Veteran Sportsman's Diary.* Sleeping in one of the keepers' bothies, having been out late the day before and not returned to the lodge, he was woken in the morning by the keeper, telling him that a bunch of stags were grazing in the vicinity of the house. Taking up his rifle, and still attired in his nightshirt, he shot one of the stags from the front door of the bothy, then went back to bed. Perhaps Prince Albert would have approved. Deer were certainly much thinner on the ground at that time – Ackroyd had a system whereby the estate shepherds would come to alert him if any stags were seen – so perhaps he could claim, with some justification, that he was simply taking advantage of an opportunity not likely to be repeated.

Although the Victorians prided themselves on their sportsmanship they were not above taking the most unfair advantage of their neighbours when chance allowed. The Duke of Portland used his keepers to drive the deer off his own ground on to the neighbouring Suisgill forest in the spring, and employed men to patrol the border of his Langwell estate where it marched with Suisgill, keeping the deer on the Suisgill ground until just before the start of the stalking season. A bothy was built out on the march for this express purpose. When the deer were finally allowed back, they would quickly move from the over-grazed ground where they had been held on to the fresh, new growth on the Langwell side of the march. It was not a practice calculated to endear him to his neighbour, nor can living for weeks on end in a bothy, far from the nearest road have been popular among his keepers.

As the southerners began to buy estates, or to take out long leases on sporting properties, so grew an awareness of the need to manage deer in a more sensible manner than simply shooting all the biggest and best stags. Owners began to introduce stags from deer parks in the south, hoping that they would pass on their size and massive antler growth to the Highland deer. They were doomed to disappointment, however, since it is the conditions in the Highlands that restrict the size and antler development of stags – not any genetic defect. In any case, many a park stag fell victim to the rifle of a neighbouring forest as soon as he ventured over the march. The effect of the introductions are still discernible in the antler shape of some stags and, even if largely unsuccessful, the experiments signalled the direction that deer management was beginning to take.

As selective culling became more widespread so the skills of the professional stalker became more important. It is relatively easy for the amateur to select the best beast from a bunch of stags, but it is a quite different matter to pick out the worst. The stalker, living among his deer throughout the year, will know which beasts are young animals which will improve their heads if left, and which are old stags going back and perhaps best shot despite having good heads. He will know which beasts were late in casting or slow to grow their summer coats (both signs of a loss in condition), and he will know many of his stags by sight, having watched them and fed them over a number of years.

If picking the right stags to cull is a difficult task, then selecting shootable hinds from among a bunch requires even more skill. Hinds have no antlers to aid selection and must be judged on their age, coat and bodily condition. It used to be thought correct to cull yeld hinds (hinds with no calf at foot), as they were thought to be barren and therefore of no benefit to the future of the herd, but it is now known that Highland hinds will not necessarily breed every year, and that a yeld hind, not weakened by bearing and suckling a calf, is among the most likely to raise a calf successfully the following summer.

The rifle used by the modern stalker differs greatly from that which the early Victorians took to the hill. The first stalking rifles were muzzle loaders, firing a solid lead bullet with the aid of a charge of black powder. Since the velocity of the bullet was limited by the powder, the killing power of the rifle came from the size and weight of the projectile. The rifles that the early Victorians used must have been fearful brutes to fire, kicking like mules and obscuring the shooter's vision in a cloud of powder smoke. In spite of the smoke and the recoil, muzzle velocities were quite low in comparison with modern rifles. Indeed, the old stalking rifles would almost certainly fail to meet the legal minimum requirements, now in force, for rifles to be used against deer.

The relatively low muzzle velocities meant that there was a very rapid drop in the bullet's trajectory, therefore judgement of range was vital if a shot was to be successful. Add to this that all shooting was done with open sights and it becomes easier to understand why so many deer were missed or wounded, particularly by inexperienced riflemen. A modern stalking rifle, with its flat trajectory and telescopic sight, can be a precise instrument even in the hands of a complete novice, but the old fashioned muzzle loaders demanded real skill from their users, a skill that was not easily acquired from the occasional shot.

It was typical of man's inbuilt resistance to change in any form that as each advance in technology improved rifles, ammunition and sights so each was dismissed, in some quarters, as unsporting. Breech-loading rifles, high-velocity ammunition, soft-nosed bullets which expanded on impact and, especially, telescopic sights were denounced as taking the skill and challenge out of deer stalking. Telescopic sights made it 'impossible to miss' according to some critics – a statement which everyone who uses a rifle will know all too well to be false. Expanding bullets meant that a shot which was slightly off target could still kill a stag instead of allowing him to escape with a wound from which he might suffer a long and painful death, but they too were considered to be making stalking too easy. Despite outcry and condemnation at the time, all these things have long since come to be accepted as normal. Few deer will now be shot with an open-sighted rifle and the use of soft-nosed or expanding ammuntion has become a legal requirement.

Two world wars had an inevitable effect on life in the deer forests, denuding the Highlands of many of the younger keepers, greatly reducing the demand for stalking and seeing a build up of vermin on the largely un-keepered ground. Indeed, much of the north of Scotland was closed to the public and given over to commando training. In more recent years there has been a considerable reduction in the numbers of men employed as stalkers, keepers and ghillies – an inevitable result of spiralling wages. In the fifties and sixties, a young man who wished to become a keeper or stalker would have little difficulty in finding employment, and assuming that his keenness did not evaporate when he discovered the reality of a keeper's life, he might reasonably have assumed that he had a trade to last him a lifetime.

Nowadays, there are far more aspirant keepers and stalkers than there are situations, and every job that is advertised can expect to meet with a flood of applicants, some better qualified than others. Despite the numbers of men and women wanting to become keepers there are probably fewer people working at the trade than at any other time this century. Estates which would once have employed a head stalker, two or three under-stalkers, a couple of pony men, a dog boy and a brace of ghillies now make do with a single-handed stalker. He may have the use of a Land Rover and perhaps some sort of all-terrain vehicle for getting round his patch, but one man, no matter how willing, can never do the work of ten.

Man has hunted the red deer for thousands of years, sometimes for sport, sometimes as a necessity for his survival. His methods have changed over the centuries, to accommodate more efficient ways of coming to terms with his quarry (as when the bow replaced the spear and was itself replaced by the firearm), and to meet the dictates of the current fashion. He has pursued the deer with hounds, hunted them afoot and from horseback, trapped them, snared them, shot them and driven them into pounds. Now, at the end of the twentieth century, no one is driven by hunger or the need to survive. The stalker, be he professional or amateur, goes to the hill because he chooses to do so, because he needs to satisfy some basic hunting instinct in his make up.

There are good, sound reasons why it is necessary to exert some sort of control over the red deer population. Even those who are opposed to all forms of what

A good stag, but one that is 'going back', and would be a suitable cull beast.

they call 'blood sports' will agree with this. Left to themselves they would wreak havoc on farmlands and many thousand deer would die from starvation every winter. The modern stalker tries to take a balanced cull from the herds, weeding out the weak and the old, leaving a healthier and stronger population to perpetuate the species. It is a far cry from the mass slaughters of old when Highlanders would kill every beast they were able to trap within their enclosures, irrespective of age, sex or state of health. Now there is a planned level of culling, careful selection of beasts to be shot and a policy of improving

Hinds and calves during a harsh winter. It takes a real expert to select the right beasts for culling from such a bunch.

the overall quality of the herds by leaving the biggest and best stags to breed and eliminating what the stalker will refer to as 'rubbish'.

Deer management is a far more scientific operation now than ever in the past. The red deer has been studied in great detail, particularly on the island of Rhum which is owned and managed by the Nature Conservancy Council. Deer farms have been started, initially in New Zealand but also in Britain, in recent years and a great deal of data has been amassed about the life cycle and natural history of these beasts. Laws have been passed for their protection while alive and an increasing number of regulations govern what may be done with the carcase of a dead animal.

Amid all these rules and regulations, all this accumulation of scientific data and application of sound management principles, one thing has not changed. When a sportsman sets out to the hill to stalk a stag, he still feels the same thrill of anticipation that his predecessors must have known. When he eases cautiously to within range of the beast his heart will beat a little faster; he will feel the same bitter disappointment at a chance bungled, the same mixture of triumph and remorse when a stalk is successfully concluded.

We stalk because we choose to do so; for the thrill of the game rather than in response to any pressure for survival. The caveman edging to within stabbing distance of his quarry was doubtless motivated by different reasons; the deer represented survival to him – the difference between life and death for himself and his family. A far greater imperative certainly, but who would doubt that, in the moment when we squeeze the trigger we are perhaps closer to the caveman hurling his spear than we might like to think, despite thousands of years of progress? As to whether that is a comforting or disturbing thought, I must leave the reader to judge.

3

Rifles and Ammunition

The equipment the stalker takes to the hill is largely a matter of personal choice. There are certain basic requirements without which no stalking is possible but after that everything is more or less optional. The rifle and ammunition are indispensable. There is no way in which a deer may be killed legally without these, the use of arrows, crossbow bolts, spears, air rifles and the like having been banned by act of parliament. It is still legal to use a shotgun to kill deer under certain circumstances (*see* Chapter 12), though such a weapon would not be used when deer stalking for sport.

Having equipped ourselves with weapon and ammunition there is nothing else that is absolutely essential in order to stalk, but high on any stalker's list of priorities would be a telescope or pair of binoculars, in order to be able to spot and identify a shootable beast and a knife to gralloch it with. Add a stick and a length of rope (in case the beast has to be dragged to the pony, Argocat, Snowtrac or whatever means is to be used to bring it to the deer larder) and there is very little else that the well-equipped stalker could desire. I have not mentioned clothing in this list as I intend to look at clothing for the hill more fully later. There are a number of other items that you may like to take to the hill with you, mainly concerned with comfort or safety, but these are definitely optional and we can consider them after taking a look at the basic necessities.

Highland stalking is a sport of the open hill, and shots may have to be taken at a considerable range.

A modern bolt-actioned stalking rifle, matched here with a 4X to 10X variable power telescopic sight.

THE RIFLE

The complete novice will probably be using the estate, or the stalker's own, rifle. This is the normal arrangement, and many experienced stalkers never own a rifle, always making use of that provided by their host. It is unlikely that you will want to purchase a rifle until you have sampled stalking for yourself. Indeed, the issue of a firearms certificate for sporting purposes will almost certainly be conditional on the police approving the area where you intend to use the weapon, the certificate then limiting use of the rifle to within that specified area. You are most unlikely to be granted a certificate for a full-bore rifle unless you have some definite arrangement about its use. In practice this is no bar to the novice who wants to try his hand at stalking and if he subsequently becomes hooked on the sport and decides that he would like his own rifle then the experience may be of assistance in obtaining a certificate.

A stalking rifle, like so many things in life, has to be a compromise between several incompatible ideals. Obviously, accuracy must be a factor when choosing a rifle which is to be used against a live target. The object of deer stalking is not simply to kill deer, but to do it as cleanly and humanely as possible. Highland deer stalking, being a sport of the open hill, means that shots may have to be taken at quite considerable range and obviously a rifle which will be consistently accurate at that range is essential. However, the most accurate rifles available, as used in full-bore competition shooting, are far too heavy and unwieldy to take to the hill. Our first compromise, therefore, is to sacrifice a little bit of accuracy to keep the weight of the weapon within reasonable limits.

This is not actually such a sacrifice as it might appear at first consideration. A modern rifle firing standard, factory-loaded ammunition, should be capable of firing a two-inch group at a hundred yards. That is well within the margins of error that should ensure a clean kill. So we needn't burden ourselves with twenty pounds of super-accurate hardware as we set off for the hill. This will certainly please the professional stalker, because he is normally the one who will carry the rifle. On the other hand, the rifle may well have to put up with some fairly rough handling, being dragged along the ground, through rocks and burns and perhaps bumping about in the back of an Argocat on the way to and from the stalking beat, so it must be of pretty robust construction, and lightweight and robustness are not always compatible.

There are further compromises to be made when we begin to consider what calibre rifle is best suited to our task. We must compromise between power and what recoil is acceptable; between bullet weight and trajectory and between rate of fire and inherent accuracy and reliability. Before looking at all these points in more detail, however, perhaps we should examine the different designs of rifle available today.

The actions available may be broadly divided into six categories: bolt-action, single-shot, lever-action, pump-action, semi-automatic and double-barrelled rifles. Inevitably, there are factors in favour of and against each, some more theoretical than practical. The prospective purchaser of a stalking rifle must consider several options before making his final choice and among these will be accuracy, reliability, safety, rate of fire, strength, availability and price. In addition, such things as the purchaser's personal preference for a particular action or maker, tradition, and the acceptance by others of something that is different from the norm, may be important.

A bolt-actioned rifle can be seen to be safe simply by opening the bolt. The magazine and chamber are both empty.

By far the majority of rifles used for stalking in the Highlands are bolt-action magazine rifles. The bolt action is a strong, simple and well-proven design. It allows a second and subsequent shots to be taken in fairly rapid succession if this should be necessary, is very reliable, easily maintained and acceptable everywhere. There is a general agreement that the bolt action is more accurate than any of the other forms of repeating rifle. While this is probably strictly correct in theory it is questionable whether the slight difference in accuracy between it and, say, a lever-actioned rifle would have any real effect on the user's success in the field. Stags are generally missed because of inadequacies in the rifleman; rarely because of any inherent defect in the rifle.

While the supposed extra fraction of accuracy may be only of theoretical benefit under field conditions, the bolt action has one or two definite advantages over lever- or pump-actioned rifles. There are fewer moving parts, and therefore fewer parts that can go wrong and the job of cleaning and maintenance is much simpler. It can be shown to be safe, i.e. unloaded, simply by opening the bolt and the bolt can be easily removed and stored separately from the rifle for security reasons. The intending purchaser of a stalking rifle will find a far wider choice of bolt actions than any other type in Britain. (Lever actions are much more common in some other countries, notably America.) The amount and variety of rifles available also means that there are prices to suit most pockets.

The dominance of the bolt-action rifle is such that it is quite rare to find any other type of weapon in use on the hill. This preponderance is, perhaps, a little surprising given the relative popularity of the various actions of .22 rimfire rifles. All the aforementioned actions, with the exception of double-barrelled rifles, are common in .22 calibre rifles and all are in regular use for sporting purposes against small game and for vermin control. Despite this general acceptance of all types of small-bore rifle, the bolt action is almost totally predominant among full-bore sporting weapons. It can be, without doubt, an excellent tool for the job, but its advantages over the other rifle actions are certainly not so outstanding as to explain this completely.

There are still some single-shot sporting rifles available on the market. At least one manufacturer offers an elegant, functional and well-finished weapon for sale in a variety of calibres. Obviously, any single-shot weapon is at a disadvantage on those occasions when a second shot may need to be taken quickly, and for this reason alone many stalkers will avoid single-shot rifles. It is not that a practised user cannot keep up a very respectable rate of fire with a single-shot rifle, but that the stalker is not usually in a state of readiness for rapid fire. With a magazine rifle the stalker reloads simply by working the bolt or lever and the weapon is instantly ready to fire. The sequence for reloading a single shot – action opened, spent round ejected, fresh round inserted, action closed – will only take a fraction longer, provided the fresh round is readily available to hand. If it is tucked away in a pocket or pouch somewhere then a long delay may occur while the rifleman tries to remember exactly which pocket it is in, and then attempts to get hold of it with frozen fingers, all while lying face down in a peat hag while the wounded beast gets away. I suppose an alternative would be to have a couple of spare rounds out ready before taking the shot, but as well as being a negative attitude, it would be one more thing to remember in the last moments of the stalk – a time when the average man has more than enough to occupy his mind anyway. If you have a particular reason for favouring a single-shot rifle then no doubt a system could be devised to keep spare rounds easily available. A short cartridge holder worn around the wrist under the coat sleeve might be satisfactory, but you will be putting one more obstacle in your path.

The lever action is widely used in other countries, but is rarely seen on a Highland hill. My local gun shop actually has a lever-actioned stalking rifle in stock and Colin, the owner, told me, rather resignedly, that he expected to have the same gun in fifty years time. While in theory the lever action is marginally less accurate than the bolt action the difference is not sufficient to account for its lack of popularity. A lever-action rifle is slightly quicker to use than a bolt-action rifle since only two movements are required to operate a lever compared to four movements with a bolt.

The lever, which forms an extension to the trigger guard, is held in the hand as the shot is taken. Two movements – one to depress the lever and a second to return it to its original position – eject the fired round, place a live round in the chamber and cock the weapon ready to fire again. With a bolt the sequence is: remove right hand from firing position to grasp and lift bolt, pull bolt back to eject spent round, push bolt forward and down to replace it with a live round and cock the action, replace right hand in firing position. It is a very slight difference but, in this respect, the lever action has a slight but definite advantage over the bolt action.

As with the question of relative accuracy, it is debatable how important this increase in the maximum rate of fire would be under field conditions. Rapid fire should be very much the exception rather than the rule when deer stalking – the aim of the stalker is always to kill with his first shot – but sooner or later everyone who stalks will wound a beast, and then the ability to get a second and third shot away quickly may make the difference between making amends for one's mistake almost immediately and a long, hard slog after a wounded deer. It should be unnecessary to add that minimising the animal's suffering is of paramount importance.

The lever-action rifle is considerably more complicated than a bolt-action rifle and this inevitably means that it is more prone to mechanical failure. The more parts there are, the more parts can go wrong. The chamber is concealed within the action body and therefore cannot be easily inspected to ensure that the rifle is not loaded – an important safety check, simple with a bolt action. If the rifle has a tube magazine you will be limited in the type of ammunition you can use since the bullets lie nose to tail in the tube. Pointed bullets, where the point of each round rests against the primer of the one in front, are definitely not to be recommended. A final consideration that may influence the choice of weapon is that the lever-action rifle may have a lower resale value than a bolt-action rifle.

Pump-actioned rifles, where the functions of ejection, reloading and cocking the firing pin are carried out by movement of the fore-end, are even less

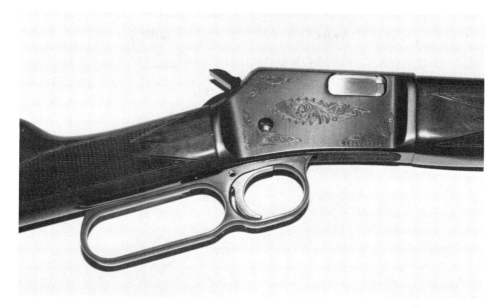

A lever-actioned rifle – actually a .22, not a stalking rifle.

common than lever-actioned weapons. Though as fast as a lever, or possibly slightly faster, to operate, they have one disadvantage particularly applicable to Highland stalking. The great majority of shots are taken in the prone position, usually with the left hand (in a right-handed shot), resting on a heathery knoll, or perhaps on the rolled-up rifle cover or the telescope case. Both a bolt action and a lever action can be operated by the right hand only, keeping the rifle in position for the the second and subsequent shots. Operating the pump action, with the necessary movement of the left hand will obviously disturb the firing position of the shooter and more than negate any slight gain in speed of reloading.

The Firearms (Amendment) Act, 1988 has made the use of pump-actioned, centre-fire rifles illegal in Britain and the same applies to semi-automatic weapons which eject the spent round, chamber a new round and cock the firing pin by utilising either gases from the burning propellant or the energy of the recoil. Finally, there is the double-barrelled rifle, a few of which are still produced by makers of the best guns and rifles. In general, such rifles, although among the most aesthetically pleasing of all hunting weapons, are prohibitively expensive. There are technical problems associated with making both barrels shoot to the same point of aim, though this is not the primary cause of the high price of such weapons. It is because, like best shotguns, double rifles are individually built, by hand, from the very best materials. They may be an excellent investment, and for those who can afford to buy them and use them on the hill, they are beautiful rifles; but it is quite unlikely that the average stalker is ever going to encounter one.

The double rifle was, and perhaps still is, popular among hunters of dangerous game, since it offers not only an almost instantaneous second shot but also a degree of insurance against mechanical defect, as the action is duplicated for each barrel. It is a rare happening for the action of a modern rifle to fail. For it to happen just at the moment when one is being confronted by a wounded and angry lion or buffalo would be misfortune of the very worst kind. If you have that kind of luck you would probably be well advised to stick to chess or tiddly-winks and give all deadly weapons a wide berth.

That, briefly, is a summary of the main types of weapon which are available to the stalker today. In practice, it is almost certain that the rifle used will be a bolt-actioned weapon; the design that has proved best for the job by reason of its accuracy, strength, reliability and ease of use since its introduction at the end of the last century. Having settled on the choice of action for our rifle we must next decide on its calibre (the size of bullet which it will fire), which leads us now to consider the ammunition we are to use.

AMMUNITION

It is only comparatively recently that there has been any legislation to govern the type of ammunition which may be used to kill deer. In the past, deer were shot with .22 rifles and with shotguns loaded with totally inadequate shot sizes and a great deal of unnecessary suffering was inflicted on animals. Even today, despite the legislation, there are those who persist in trying to kill red deer with .22 rifles. The agony which must be suffered by a beast whose jaw has been shattered by a misplaced shot from a poacher defies imagination. A deer wounded in this way, and it is all too common, is probably condemned to a lingering death from starvation. I say 'probably' because on occasion, as I have seen for myself, the jaw eventually heals sufficiently for the beast to eat again, but the pain and hunger suffered in the intervening period must be truly unbearable.

Slightly different rules govern what ammunition may be used to shoot deer according to whether the stalker is in England, Wales, Scotland, or Northern Ireland. These are explained in more detail in Chapter 12, but briefly, the requirements for red deer in Scotland are as follows. The bullet must be soft nosed, have a minimum weight of 100 grains, a minimum muzzle velocity of 2,450 feet per second and a minimum muzzle energy of 1,750 foot pounds. Obviously then, the first requirement of our ammunition is that it should conform with these legal minima.

With ammunition, as with the rifle itself, it is necessary to compromise. There are two requirements to be met if it is to be satisfactory for the deer stalker's purpose. Firstly, it must be possible for him to place the bullet, with certainty, in one of the vulnerable areas of a deer at all normal stalking ranges. Secondly, the bullet must reach the deer with sufficient energy remaining to ensure a quick and humane kill, provided that the shot is accurate.

'Normal stalking range' is a nice, glib phrase that obviously requires some amplification, since it is vital to both requirements. It is always dangerous to generalise, but it is probably safe to say that the majority of deer stalked in the Highlands are shot at ranges of between fifty and two hundred and fifty yards.

Red deer stags in early spring. An animal the size of a stag requires a bullet of considerable power to ensure a clean and swift kill.

We could almost certainly narrow that range further to between a hundred and a hundred and fifty yards, but circumstances may dictate that a closer, or longer shot is unavoidable, and our ammunition must be able to cope with the extremes.

Having quantified our range, albeit rather loosely, we can begin to narrow down the requirements of our ammunition. If we are using a well-made rifle, and for the moment we ignore wind drift, it is the trajectory of the bullet that will largely determine how accurate our shooting can be. Bullets, unfortunately, do not travel in straight lines. If we have sighted our rifle in at, say, one hundred yards, then at that distance, the bullet should strike the target at exactly the point where the sights indicate. At any distance less than one hundred yards, apart from a few feet immediately in front of the muzzle, the bullet will strike somewhere above the aiming point, and for all distances beyond one hundred yards it will strike somewhere below; the distance below increasing as the range increases.

The reason for this is that, for all practical purposes, a bullet is dropping under the influence of gravity from the moment it leaves the muzzle. The further from the muzzle the more rapid the drop relative to forward motion. This drop can be calculated exactly and tables are available which predict the drop of any given bullet, provided that the muzzle velocity and ballistic coefficient are known. Ballistic coefficient is the Sectional Density divided by the Form Factor of the bullet. Sectional Density is the weight of the bullet (in pounds) divided by its diameter (in inches) squared. Form Factor deals with the bullet shape and how well it overcomes air resistance.

Three stalking rounds, from left to right: 7mm Remington Magnum, .270 Winchester and .243 Winchester. At either end, two illegal rounds for comparison: a 12-bore shot gun cartridge and a .22 long rifle.

End on view: 12 bore, 7mm Remington Magnum, .270 Winchester, .243 Winchester and .22.

However, for any given ballistic coefficient, the higher the muzzle velocity the flatter the trajectory. Put more simply, with our rifle sighted in at one hundred yards for a particular cartridge, the faster that the bullet leaves the muzzle the less will be the distance above the aiming point at which the bullet strikes the target at ranges less than one hundred yards; and the less the distance below the aiming point at distances greater than one hundred yards.

There are tables published which list this in some detail. For instance, when fired from a rifle sighted in at one hundred yards a .243 Winchester 100-grain bullet, having a muzzle velocity of 3,070 feet per second, will be 2.9 inches low at two hundred yards and 10.6 inches low at three hundred yards. The same ammunition fired from a rifle sighted in at two hundred yards will strike the target 1.4 inches high at one hundred yards and 6.3 inches low at three hundred. If we had the same bullet, but with a muzzle velocity of only 2,000 feet per second, then our rifle sighted in at one hundred yards would shoot 7.5 inches low at two hundred yards and 26.5 inches low at three hundred. With the rifle sighted at two hundred yards the figures are: 4.5 inches high at one hundred yards and 15.8 inches low at three hundred.

So what is the importance of a flat trajectory? Unlike the target shot, the stalker cannot be certain of what range he will be firing at. Since the range cannot be predetermined we must either have a bullet with a flat trajectory, or begin making adjustments in our aiming point to compensate for differences in range. In addition, there is no way to check the actual distance from you to the stag; it has to be an estimate. Given a flat enough trajectory and a correctly sighted rifle, we can simply ignore differences in the striking point of the bullet across the normal stalking ranges.

Obviously we need the highest muzzle velocity we can get, combined with the highest ballistic coefficient, in order to get the flattest possible trajectory. If only it were that simple. Let us leave the question of trajectory aside for the moment and consider the factors needed to ensure that our ideal bullet gives us a quick and humane kill.

When a rifle is fired, the propellant is ignited and imparts energy to the bullet. The energy is converted into motion and the bullet leaves the barrel, spinning, because the rifle has spiral grooves along the length of the barrel imparting directional stability. Once clear of the barrel, the bullet proceeds to expend its energy in overcoming the effects of gravity and wind resistance until such time as it either strikes something or, having expended all its energy, falls to the ground.

In our case, and provided we have pointed the rifle in the right direction, the bullet should strike a stag or a hind somewhere in the first fifty to two hundred and fifty yards of its flight and discharge its remaining energy within the body of the beast, thus rendering it quickly and humanely dead. The energy contained in our bullet is the product of its velocity and its mass. Having made decisions about the velocity of our bullet we must now decide on its ideal size. We should then have defined the perfect projectile for deer stalking. Maybe; but first a word or two about the bullet itself.

The law demands that all ammunition used for the killing of deer must be soft nosed. This is to ensure that the bullet will expand when it strikes the deer making a considerably larger wound than would a fully jacketed bullet such as those used in military rifles. The fully jacketed bullet would pass right through a deer's body and continue on its way having expended only a part of its energy on the deer. A soft point expands and sometimes breaks up as it enters the animal's body, causing much greater damage and a far more quick and certain death.

Ideally, the bullet should expend all its energy within the body of the animal but, in practice, this does not always happen. The range at which the shot is taken will obviously affect the energy remaining when the beast is struck. The point of impact – whether it is bone or soft tissue – will alter the way in which the bullet expands and the size of the beast itself will vary. The law sets out the minimum energy which our bullet must have. As we shall see, there are various factors which set practical limits on the maximum energy which is desirable.

The saying 'you don't get owt for nowt' is true of most things in life and ballistics are no exception. To alter the amount of energy a bullet has, we must change either its size or its velocity. A larger bullet will require a larger charge of propellant to maintain its velocity; a smaller bullet will gain in velocity, but will still require a larger charge if it is to compensate for its reduction in mass and still reach the target with increased energy. However, according to Newton's laws, for every action there is an equal and opposite reaction. Increase the charge to increase the energy which is imparted to the bullet and, inevitably, you will also increase the recoil and the muzzle blast.

When a rifle is fired, the burning propellant drives the bullet forwards out of the muzzle and at the same time tries to drive the rifle backwards as the rear of the cartridge case slams against the action face. The bullet, weighing perhaps a 100 grains, leaves the muzzle at some 3,000 feet per second; the rifle, weighing perhaps seven pounds, moves backwards with the same energy, but with considerably less velocity. However, the higher the energy with which the bullet leaves the muzzle, the harder the force of the recoil, and it is the stalker's shoulder which has to absorb that recoil.

We can, of course, reduce the apparent recoil by increasing the weight of the rifle. The heavier the rifle, the greater the inertia which has to be overcome to start it moving backwards, therefore the lower the recoil perceived by the shooter. But remember that you have to carry that rifle around on your shoulder and you may be walking several miles over steep and rough country.

In any case, there is no point in using a bullet that has more than the necessary amount of energy which will ensure a quick, clean kill if it is properly placed. Too powerful a cartridge might increase the amount of damage done to the carcase – a waste of some of the best meat that money can buy – and carries the risk of wounding other beasts which are in the vicinity of the original target. Once the bullet has expanded, or possibly fragmented, on impact, there is no guarantee that it will continue in the same, or even approximately the same, path when it leaves the body of the beast at which it was fired. Other deer standing in the general area are liable to be wounded and it is quite possible that such an injury goes unnoticed by the stalkers, leaving the wounded beast to suffer.

To summarise, we need a bullet with a reasonably flat trajectory, sufficient energy to ensure a clean kill and an acceptable level of recoil. The provisions of the law ensure that nobody should go to the hill armed with a rifle that fails to meet the requirements of energy and muzzle velocity, but the stalker can choose from a number of calibres and bullet weights which are both legally and practically acceptable.

An important consideration when purchasing a rifle, particularly a second-hand rifle, is whether the ammunition is easily available and will continue to be available in the future. There are many calibres of rifle on the market, many of which will meet the legal requirements for red deer stalking. However, ammunition for some of the more unusual calibres may be difficult or almost impossible to obtain, and prohibitively expensive into the bargain. Anyone contemplating the purchase of a stalking rifle would be well advised to consider one of the four or five most popular calibres, thus ensuring an easy supply of ammunition for the foreseeable future.

The four most common calibres in current use are probably the .243 Winchester, the .270 Winchester, the .308 and the 7mm. Of these the most popular (in the north of Scotland anyway), are the .243 and the .270. The .270 is a considerably bigger cartridge and packs a correspondingly harder punch, though at the expense of greater recoil and noise. The .243 has the flatter trajectory of the two, but the difference is very slight.

As to which is the better rifle, this is very much a matter of personal choice. I have two books on my shelves whose authors try to make an objective choice of the best calibre rifle for deer. One makes out an excellent case for the .243, citing flat trajectory, low recoil, low muzzle blast and ample killing power as his reasons. The other author rejects the .243 almost out of hand, preferring the .270 with its greater killing power, wider choice of bullet weights... but it is unnecessary to go on. Both are excellent calibres for red deer. Both will do the job quite adequately if correctly aimed, and choice between the two is largely a matter of personal preference.

Talking to some of the local professional stalkers, the following points were made, though not all agreed on the same things. The .243 is the rifle of choice for hind stalking, but the extra power of the .270 is preferable when the larger size and weight of stags is taken into consideration. The lower muzzle blast of the .243 creates less disturbance on the hill and the lower recoil allows for more accurate shooting with less risk of flinching. The .243 is quite adequate in the hands of a good rifle shot, but the .270 gives a slightly increased margin of error if the shooter is a little wayward. A .243 can be built rather lighter and is therefore easier to carry. I list the points out of interest since they may help in the choice of a rifle.

Both calibres meet all the requirements discussed earlier, as do the .308, the 7mm and indeed several other calibres such as the .275 Rigby, the .257 Weatherby Magnum and the .257 Roberts. In the end the choice of calibre must be a matter of individual preference and the half dozen I have mentioned are far from an exhaustive list. There are a number of other calibres on the market which will meet all the stalker's requirements.

A good gun shop will carry a range of stalking rifles, and can advise the novice on which is most suitable for his particular sport.

One point well worth consideration when purchasing a rifle is the other uses to which it may be put besides red deer stalking. If the stalker also has access to roe stalking then the .243 might be a better choice than one of the heavier calibres. Loaded with a 50-grain bullet it is an excellent roe rifle, though, of course, not then legal for red deer where the minimum bullet weight is 100 grains. If your ambitions run to elk stalking in one of the Scandinavian countries, a heavier calibre might well be indicated.

Whatever the sportsman's final choice, it will inevitably represent some sort of compromise. There are many combinations of bore size and bullet weight that will deal adequately with the red deer of the Highlands, but as yet there is no one combination that is unarguably superior to all others. Choose the one that seems to suit you best, practise until you develop real confidence in it, then use it and enjoy it. There is no such thing as the right rifle for everybody; just the right rifle for you.

4

Sights, Scopes and Sticks

SIGHTS

It is not enough simply to choose a combination of rifle and ammunition which can deliver a bullet of sufficient power and with acceptable accuracy to ensure a clean kill at normal stalking ranges. The sighting system on the rifle must also be suitable for hill stalking. It must complement the accuracy of the rifle, be quick and easy to use, light and easy to carry and robust enough to stand up to both the recoil of the rifle and the wear and tear which is an inevitability of stalking in the Highlands.

In the Victorian era virtually all stalkers used open sights. Since the rifles (particularly in the earlier years of the nineteenth century), were not very accurate and their low muzzle velocities gave them a looping trajectory, there was little point in anything more refined than simple iron sights. As the power and accuracy of rifles improved, so the need for a more precise sighting system became apparent and the telescopic sight gradually phased out the old-fashioned open sight. Predictably, this move was not met with universal favour. Telescopic sights were not considered sporting since they were supposed to make the task of correct bullet placement too easy. It was a strange attitude, though perhaps typical of the times.

Inaccurate sights might cause a miss, or far worse, a wounded beast – something no stalker should ever risk unnecessarily. The skill in deer stalking lies in getting to within range of the deer, not in making a difficult shot which, by definition, means an increased chance of wounding a beast. Anything that lessens that chance must be good for the sport. Despite this, telescopic sights were commonly dismissed as unsporting. It was this same type of thinking that, a few years later was to deny the use of parachutes to Royal Flying Corps pilots on the grounds that such equipment might encourage them to abandon their planes when under attack. Man seems to have an inbuilt resistance to change. Did the cavemen dismiss the bow and arrow as unsporting I wonder?

In some respects, open sights still have a place in the deer stalker's armoury. They are quite a lot quicker to use than a telescopic sight and much less prone to damage from knocks and recoil. Where the range at which they will be used is limited – in woodland stalking, for example – they may be preferred by some stalkers. On the open hills of the Highlands, however, the telescopic sight has found almost universal favour. Even so, it is perhaps worth looking briefly at the types of open sights which are still used before considering telescopic sights in more detail.

An old Mannlicher-Schonaeur 6.5mm rifle, with both aperture and open, iron sights.

The simplest form of open sight consists of a blade on the front of the barrel which is aligned with a notch in the rear sight, fixed further back along the barrel. There is usually some means of raising and lowering the rear sight to control the elevation of the bullet strike and some rifles have a means of moving the rear sight from side to side to control the azimuth (the distance to the side of the point of aim the bullet strikes). This is the quickest type of sight to use and is the type usually fitted to the rifle when it leaves the manufacturer.

It has the advantage of being very robust, of minimal cost, and having virtually nothing which can go wrong. To use it, however, requires that the eye should focus simultaneously on three points: the rear sight, the front sight and the target. This, sadly, is impossible. What the eye can do is to change focus between each of the three points very rapidly – so rapidly that all three appear to be in focus at the same time. Unfortunately, as the shooter grows older, this ability of the eye to flicker back and forth with its focussing distance is progressively lost. As this happens so the degree of accuracy which can be obtained with open sights also fades.

Using the second type of open sight – the aperture, or peep sight – will overcome this to some extent. This consists of a blade or bead front sight which is aligned through a tiny hole in the rear sight, fixed to the rifle so as to be close to the shooter's eye. The eye, looking through the hole, has only to focus on two points simultaneously – the bead and the target – which makes sighting a little simpler as far as the eye is concerned. Aperture sights are capable of far greater accuracy at long range than simple open sights and are used by competitors in target rifle competitions. The rear sight is usually adjustable for both elevation and windage (azimuth), and may offer a choice of aperture sizes to suit differing conditions of visibility. On the other hand, the rear sight is slightly more prone to accidental damage and is considerably slower in use since the 'picture' which the eye sees through the peep-hole is necessarily very restricted. In experienced hands, an aperture sight can be both quick to use and very accurate, but the first choice of virtually all hill stalkers today is some type of telescopic sight.

The telescopic sight is normally fitted above the breech of the rifle, though on rare occasions it may be fitted to one side, for example, when the rifle action ejects spent cartridge cases through the top of the breech. It magnifies the target, giving it the appearance of being closer than it actually is, and superimposes some form of sighting reference on top of the magnified image. Since the image and the sighting reference (called the reticles), are in the same optical plane, both will appear in sharp focus at the same time, provided the sight is properly adjusted.

There are a number of reputable makers of telescopic sights advertising in the shooting press and the purchaser has a wide choice of model and price. Sights are usually described by two figures – one representing the degree of magnification which the sight gives and the other representing the diameter of the object lens, i.e. 6X40. The higher the first figure, the greater the magnification of the target; the higher the second figure, the larger the front lens of the sight and, therefore, the greater its light gathering power. The larger the object lens, the brighter the image, and the better the sight will perform in poor light, though generally these improvements will also be reflected in the price.

Initially at least, magnification is probably of more importance when choosing a 'scope than any of the other variables. There are 'scopes made which offer 1X magnification – the image appears the same size through the 'scope as when seen by the naked eye – but these will not normally be used for Highland

Checking the rifle before going to the hill. The stalker steadies his telescope against his stick to monitor the strike of the bullet on the target.

A selection of telescopic sights suitable for deer stalking.

stalking where the Rifle will usually be shooting at ranges where some degree of magnification is a definite asset. At the other end of the scale, anything over 10X magnification is probably too high for use on the hill, for reasons which we will see in a moment.

The degree of magnification also represents the apparent reduction in the distance from the rifle to the target. A stag standing one hundred yards away will appear to be fifty yards away through a 2X 'scope and twenty-five yards away through a 4X instrument. It might seem, therefore, that the greater the degree of magnification the easier the stalker's task – fit a 25X 'scope and a stag two hundred yards away will appear to be only eight yards distant and therefore be un-missable. It all sounds too easy, and there is, inevitably, a price to be paid for all that magnification.

The higher the magnification, the narrower the field of view, and there is no way around it. As the field of view (the angle through which the 'scope sees) narrows, it becomes progressively more difficult to use. The small sight picture makes it difficult to locate the target and the higher magnification exaggerates any tiny movement of the rifle making it apparently harder to hold steady. With a very high magnification 'scope such as the 25X or 30X, which target shooters use, it would be very difficult to locate the stag or hind at all, or to be sure that the correct beast was being selected if it was one of a group. Lower magnification shows a broader picture, both the target beast and its immediate surroundings being visible – an important factor to ensure that there is not a second animal standing in line with the one to be shot.

Another problem with high magnification telescopic sights is that eye relief becomes increasingly critical as the degree of magnification rises. When you look through a properly set up 'scope sight you should see a bright, clear image filling the whole of the viewing lens. If you move your head slightly backwards, forwards or to one side then the image will appear to decrease in size, becoming a round picture surrounded by a dark border. The amount of latitude before this vignetting occurs is the eye relief and decreases as the magnification increases. To the target shot this may actually be an advantage, ensuring that his cheek is on exactly the same place on the comb of the stock for every shot, but it is of little help to the stalker, particularly if he is lying in an awkward position, or needs to get a shot off quickly.

There are no hard and fast rules governing 'scope magnification, but in practice a magnification of between 4X and 6X would seem to be about the norm. This gives a useful degree of 'shortening' of the apparent range while still allowing a wide enough field of view to make target location quick and relatively easy. There are a number of 'scopes on the market which offer a variable degree of magnification in the manner of a zoom lens. The range available will obviously vary between manufacturers and models, but variations in the order of 3X to 9X are common. In a well made variable-power 'scope there should obviously not be any alteration in the point of aim as the magnification is changed. Variable-power sights offer a useful extra to the stalker, but there are certain reservations.

A telescopic sight is a very precise and potentially very delicate instrument, mounted on a rifle that is subject to a sudden and violent recoil every time that it is fired. The slightest movement of the mounts, the reticles or of the sight itself will have a far greater effect on the point of impact of the bullet. The necessary refinements for variable power mean that there are yet more pieces to be subjected to the recoil and, therefore, more pieces that can go wrong. In addition, I suspect that after the first few days of use, many variable-power 'scopes will simply be set on the most convenient compromise setting and left there for the rest of their lives. However, if you want a variable-power telescopic sight and your pocket can afford it, then there are no overriding reasons for choosing a fixed-power model in preference.

We have already touched on the subject of recoil and this brings us to another requirement of a telescopic sight for use with a stalking rifle. It must be strong enough to stand the constant recoil of the rifle without any alteration at all in its point of aim. The cheaper models of 'scope sight which are meant for use on air rifles and .22 rifles are most definitely not suitable for use with a stalking rifle. They are designed for weapons which have little or no recoil and will quickly be ruined if attached to a full-bore rifle, resulting perhaps in an 'inexplicable' miss or a wounded beast.

Whatever degree of magnification is selected, the purchaser of a telescopic sight must also decide on the type of reticle which is to be incorporated. Here again there is a wide, not to say somewhat confusing, choice available and final selection will depend, at least in part, on personal preference. The most common styles of reticle are either cross hairs or some kind of post, plus various types of dot and combinations of some or all of these.

Again, there are no hard and fast rules as to which is the best of the various designs on offer. Post sights may offer marginally quicker sighting, particularly for short-range shooting such as occurs at times in woodland stalking, though this obviously does not apply to the usual conditions to be met on a Highland hill. Personally, I prefer cross hairs and I have a particular liking for the sort which has broad outer sections to the hairs narrowing to fine lines in the centre. This provides very precise sighting at the junction of the crossed hairs, while the broader, outer lines enable easier sighting in poor light. I don't care for post sights at all, particularly the type with a flat-topped post, and never shoot well when using a rifle so equipped. I think this is because the extra width of the post encourages me to be less precise in aiming. Also, at longer ranges the broad post will obscure much of the beast, particularly below the point of aim. However, I must stress that this is purely a personal preference. I know several stalkers who prefer a post sight, even a flat-topped post, to any form of cross hairs and are capable of very precise shooting with it.

This may not be very much in the way of practical help, particularly if you are choosing a 'scope sight with little previous experience of such instruments, but I can only repeat that, in the end, the sight you will shoot best with will be the one that suits you personally – and only experience can tell you which it is.

TELESCOPES AND BINOCULARS

Some form of telescope or binocular is almost essential to the Highland stalker. I say 'almost', since it is obviously possible to stalk successfully using only the power of the naked eye, but so doing would place the stalker under a considerable handicap. An optical device of one sort or another is used initially when spying to locate deer and to decide whether a particular beast is shootable, i.e. one that should be selected for culling. Once the stalk has begun the telescope or binoculars may be needed frequently to check that the ground in front is clear of other deer, and finally the stalker will use his 'scope to check the exact strike of the bullet when the beast is shot.

The professional stalker will always be equipped with one or the other, and sometimes with both binoculars and telescope. While not strictly necessary for

Spying a face for deer. Here both the stalker and Rifle are using telescopes well braced against their sticks for steadiness.

the amateur stalker who is to accompany the professional, a pair of binoculars will add greatly to the enjoyment of a day's stalking. In the early stages of the day, the deer which are to form the object of the stalk may well be at such a distance as to be completely invisible to the naked eye. Unless a great deal of time is to be spent either borrowing the stalker's equipment or sitting waiting while the stalker is spying, anyone who goes to the hill with a stalking party, whether as participant or spectator, is well advised to take a pair of binoculars as part of his or her equipment.

Most professional Highland stalkers will use a telescope with which to spy. A typical 'scope of 20X to 30X magnification will allow him to make a quite detailed assessment of the quality of a stag at distances as far as a mile away. A telescope is not an easy instrument to use properly, however. There are three problems. As we have seen with telescopic sights, high magnification means a narrow field of view and this can present the novice with considerable difficulties in finding deer to spy in the first place. If deer are located it can still be difficult to place them accurately when the 'scope has been removed from the eye, since the narrow field of view will not have provided a reference point in the form of nearby features. It can be infuriating to see a deer quite clearly through the telescope, turn to point out the spot to a companion, then be quite unable to indicate the position or even to find it again through the telescope. The skill can be obtained with practice, but it does take time.

Not only does a telescope have a narrow field of view, it also has a short depth of focus (or more correctly, depth of field). This is the distance between two points in the line of sight which will be in acceptably sharp focus. The higher the magnification, the narrower the depth of field and the more difficult it will be

Binoculars up to about 10X magnification can be used free-hand; a telescope nearly always needs some kind of support.

for the user to focus the glass correctly. Again, this is a technique that will improve with practice. Finally, as with all high magnification optical devices, the greater the degree of magnification the harder it is to hold the image steady. This applies to both telescopes and binoculars, but since, in general, a stalking telescope will be of three to four times the magnification of normal binoculars, it is a greater problem for the telescope user. With a draw telescope it is almost essential that the front end be braced against something firm in order to hold it still enough for satisfactory use. Stalkers use their stick, a convenient rock or clump of heather, or lay down with the scope resting on their knee or perhaps a boot. Forget all those Hollywood images of the pirate captain standing on the deck of his ship in a force-nine gale, clapping his telescope to his eye and immediately crying 'Ah Jim lad, it be a Spanish treasure ship!' The chances are that he would never even find a ship through a telescope, much less manage to see what it was.

All this is not to condemn the use of the telescope on the hill. Indeed, it is almost essential for assessing the quality of a head, or checking a group of hinds to see what may be shootable. But it must be in practised hands. For the beginner, a good or even cheap pair of binoculars will be far more useful. There is always time to add a telescope later if you wish to increase your viewing power.

Everyone should be familiar with binoculars. They are, in effect, twin telescopes, compressed in length by using a series of prisms to refract the light waves within the body, making them less unwieldy and easier to handle. Some have individual focussing for each side, but a more common arrangement is to have a central focussing ring, with one eye-piece adjustable to compensate for any differences in the user's own eyes.

Since binoculars are an optical device just like the telescope and telescopic sights, the same laws apply to them. A higher degree of magnification brings the object viewed in closer at the expense of field of view, depth of field and steadiness. Binoculars up to about 10X magnification can be held free-hand with very little difficulty; 15X magnification is quite hard to hold steady and the field of view is noticeably narrower. Anything above 20X and you are beginning to have all the problems associated with a draw telescope.

As a general guide, a magnification of between six and ten times is probably about right for Highland stalking. Binoculars, like telescopic sights, are described in terms of two figures, separated by an 'X' – 6X40, 7X50 and so on. The first figure is the degree of magnification, the second the diameter of the object lens. Again, as with sights, the larger the object lens the greater the light gathering power of the binoculars and the brighter and clearer the image should be. I say 'should be' because brightness and clarity will also depend on the quality of the lenses and prisms and the care and accuracy applied in their construction.

The price of binoculars can show some quite startling variations between apparently similar instruments. For example, you can pay as little as £10 or as much as £450 for a pair of 8X40 binoculars. Obviously there will be a vast difference in the quality of the optics, the strength and quality of construction and the finish, but there are some remarkable bargains to be found, and the most expensive instrument will not necessarily be the best. If you already own a pair

Binoculars and a monocular – a wide range of quality and price, but all suitable for the stalker.

of binoculars then they will almost certainly be suitable for use when stalking, unless they are a specially high-powered pair designed for a particular purpose such as astronomy. Take them along in any case. They will certainly be better than nothing and can always be changed for something more suitable in the future.

When buying, always remember that whatever you choose will have to be carried with you, and you may well be doing a lot of walking. Equipment slung lightly over the shoulder at nine o'clock in the morning may have assumed quite a different feel by six or seven o'clock at night, especially if you have covered twenty miles of the Highlands in between times. Those super-heavyweight 10X70 armoured binoculars which seemed so attractive in the shop may not be so popular at the end of a long day on the hill.

Large object lenses, though improving the performance of the binoculars, particularly in low light, do tend to make the glasses bulky and this can be a nuisance when you are forced to crawl during the course of a stalk. The mini-binoculars, in the 8X20 to 10X20 range are becoming popular and are seen more and more on the hill. While they are undoubtedly inferior to full-sized glasses in their optical performance, they do have the advantages of neatness and lightness. Instead of being carried in a case or slung round the neck on a strap, they can be slipped into the breast pocket of your jacket, affixed to the lapel with a lanyard to guard against accidental loss.

Worn thus they are ready for instant use and will not inconvenience the user when he is crawling. Also, the fact that this provides some degree of protection from the weather without the use of a binocular case is useful. The noise of a pair of binoculars being taken out of and replaced in their case can be quite enough to persuade deer that there is something untoward happening in their immediate vicinity and can easily result in a stalk being ruined.

As I have already suggested, there is a tremendous variation in price between different makes of binoculars, even between supposedly similar models. To a certain extent you get what you pay for, but the most expensive is not necessarily the best, though quality does undoubtedly improve broadly in line with price. If you are considering buying a very expensive pair of binoculars for stalking it is worth considering how you will feel about using your precious optics in a rain shower or a blizzard. If you are going to spend the entire stalk worrying about damaging or dirtying your glasses then you would probably have been better to have settled for a cheaper pair in the first place. As a general rule, if you avoid buying binoculars that are too powerful, too heavy, too fragile or too expensive then you will probably not go wrong.

Having got a pair of more or less expensive binoculars, or even a telescope, it is well worth while taking a little trouble to look after them properly. If you are going to use them on the hill then obviously they are going to have to put up with a certain amount of abuse – getting wet, dusty, stained with peat and perhaps suffering the occasional knock. On the other hand, there is no need to put them through more of an ordeal than is strictly necessary. Keep them dry as much as possible and try to minimise the dust, pollen and bits of heather which are attracted, as if by a magnet, to the lenses.

Dust and wet are the main enemies of lenses, but neither will do as much damage as a well-meaning attempt at cleaning, using a pocket handkerchief to scrub vigorously at the lens surfaces. This is a sure way to ruin a lens, irrespective of whether it was the best on the market or the cheapest available. Get one of the little blower brushes sold by photographic shops, plus a supply of lens cleaning fluid and lens tissues. Blow the dirt away first, then gently clean the fronts of the lens elements with tissues and a little fluid. If you bring your binoculars home wet from the hill don't just bung them in the case and forget them. Wipe the worst of the water off, taking care not to damage the lens surfaces, then leave them in a warm room to dry out naturally before putting them back into their case. Incidentally, the same goes for telescopic sights. It doesn't take long to look after your 'scopes and binoculars, and you will be rewarded with both a longer useful life and enhanced optical performance from them.

KNIVES

Knives, like binoculars, are not strictly necessary. A stalker friend of mine once discovered that he had lost his own knife somewhere in the course of a stalk. The guest who was with him that day was one of the few stalkers who didn't have a knife of his own, so a return to neolithic times was indicated and the stag was duly gralloched using a sharp stone that happened to be handy. I suppose if there hadn't been a sharp stone they could have used their teeth, but I certainly wouldn't relish that prospect, particularly with a well run stag.

You could, I suppose, rely on a sharp stone always being to hand, or indeed

Gralloching a stag. Every stalker should carry a knife with him when he goes to the hill.

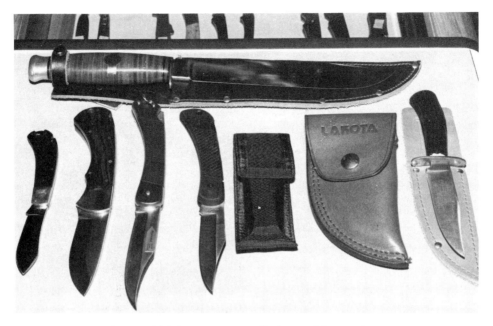

Sheath-knives, pocket-knives and belt-knives – just a small selection of the range in my local gun shop.

Bleeding a hind after a cold winter stalk. Make sure you can open your knife, even when your hands are frozen.

carry a sharp stone in your pocket. But for the sake of simplicity let us agree that at least one member of the stalking party should carry a knife somewhere about their person. If you are going to the hill with a professional stalker, and you almost certainly will be, then it is safe to assume that he will be carrying a knife. However, everyone is subject to human failings, even professional stalkers. He may forget it, lose it, or even break it and then the wisdom of carrying your own knife will become apparent.

What sort of knife should the stalker take to the hill with him? The knife is needed to gralloch the stag or hind and, depending on the method you use, may be needed to bleed it. For both purposes a single blade will suffice, provided that it is pointed (for sticking the beast to bleed it), and sharp (for slitting open the abdomen for gralloching). If it is a folding knife then it is as well to have one in which the blade locks in the open position, thus saving possible damage to the hands if the blade should inadvertently close while in use.

Practically any sort of knife will do. There is an enormous range on the market, some sold specifically as stalkers' or hunters' knives, some – like the marvellous Swiss Army range – designed to cope with practically any emergency that might beset the owner. You can pay as much as you care to invest for your knife, or indeed as little. Provided that it has a sharp, pointed blade it will probably be perfectly adequate for the task. However, this need not stop the stalker from indulging in whatever style and price of knife may suit both his fancy and his pocket.

There are pocket-knives, sheath-knives and belt-knives, the latter being folding, pocket-type knives worn in a pouch attached to the belt – a sort of hybrid between a sheath- and a penknife. Pocket-knives have a tendency to wear holes in your pockets and may then slip out and be lost, along with anything else you happen to have in the pocket. Sheath-knives, unless securely fastened, also have an unfortunate tendency to go missing when stalking. If they are kept in the sheath solely under the influence of gravity then they are liable to disappear when the owner starts to proceed down a steep face in a recumbent position. And once dropped into the heather, a knife, and anything else, is probably gone for ever.

Some of the problems can be overcome by attaching the knife to an appropriate part of clothing, or person, by means of a lanyard. Then, if your knife wears a hole in your pocket you will not lose the knife – just your car keys and whatever else may have been in the pocket with them. If it is a sheath-knife, then you may find yourself crawling along on the naked blade or stabbing yourself when you sit down, but this should at least alert you to the impending loss of the knife. Belt-knives are safer, until the pouch snaps open and the knife slips out. But take a knife along anyway. You just might need it – if only to peel your luncheon apple.

Seriously, there are some beautiful knives on the market, many designed with the stalker specifically in mind and incorporating special blades for gralloching, with rounded tips which can't puncture the stomach wall. There are knives with bone or horn grips, knives finished to specific degrees of hardness, knives inlaid with platinum or gold and knives whose price would purchase a rifle complete with telescopic sights and a box of ammunition for a less discerning stalker. They all do the job – some with rather more style than others – and give the stalker plenty of scope to suit his own preference and wallet.

If you choose a sheath-knife, avoid those with too long a blade. Three to four inches is quite adequate and far less liable to poke into your back or legs when you are crawling. Do not get a pocket-knife with a spring which makes it hard to open. If it is hard to open in the shop with warm hands think what it will be like out on the hill in January when your hands are frozen stiff. Finally, whatever you choose, keep it sharp. It does a better job that way and you will be far less likely to cut yourself.

STICKS

A stick is useful for all kinds of purposes on the hill. It is a great aid to balance, especially on steep slopes or when crossing burns. It can be used to test the softness of the ground in boggy places and it is welcome to lean on when taking a breather. It helps to steady the telescope when spying and may even be needed, on occasion, to provide a rest for the rifle, though the shot will normally be taken from the prone position. In addition, if a stag has to be dragged any distance then winding the dragging rope around a stick will make the task a lot easier on the hands.

Using a stick to ease the pressure on the hands when dragging a stag. The rope is tied around the shaft of the stick, and the stick is held across the shoulder.

Any stick will do as long as it is strong enough to bear a fair proportion of your weight and comfortable to use. Metal tips can be a nuisance, especially in rocky areas where they can alert a beast if they are allowed to bang against a stone. If you choose a stick topped with antler, particularly a thumb stick, beware of one which has sharp points on the antlers. You might fall on those points one day and cause a serious injury. When crawling, the stick is sometimes a nuisance, having to be slid along beside you as you go. I have often thought of attaching my own stick to a lanyard so I could just drag it along behind, but I've never actually bothered to do it, so I don't know how well it would work in practice.

OTHER EQUIPMENT

The list of useful, and potentially useful items that you might take to the hill with you can be as long as your imagination and ingenuity will allow. A length of rope – perhaps twenty feet of three-eighths nylon – is handy if you have to drag a beast, but the stalker will probably have already thought of that. I am taking lunch and some form of insect repellent in summer for granted. There are various safety and survival aids which you might like to have along: a compass and map spring to mind, though the professional stalker might take this as insulting to his knowledge of his patch. Tissues to clean binocular lenses, matches, some sticking plaster, a torch, one of those tin-foil survival blankets, perhaps a couple of flares, some emergency rations... You can make a list as long as you like and someone else will still be able to suggest another half dozen 'essentials'.

In the end you will be limited by what you can carry. The stalker will carry the rifle, but it is not fair to expect him to be weighted down under all your junk. You could pile it all into one of those hiker's rucksacks, but it would stick out like a sore thumb when you had to crawl. A box of matches, the tin-foil blanket and a bar of chocolate or Kendal Mint Cake will all slip into a pocket somewhere without any real inconvenience, and they might just save your life in the event of an accident. If the lack of it worries you, then take it with you; otherwise don't burden yourself down any more than necessity and common sense dictate.

5
Clothing

Highland weather is notoriously fickle and the stalker must dress to cope with the best and the worst that a day may throw at him. You may be sunburnt in January, make a snowball in June and can be drenched by a downpour on any or every day of the year. It is the speed at which a warm, sunny day can become cold and wet that makes the selection of clothing for the hill difficult. Early morning may be shirt-sleeve weather as the sun burns away the mist, but the memory of that warmth will be of little comfort if cloud and rain roll in from the west later, particularly if by then the stalking party is three thousand feet up a mountain and ten miles from home. Not only may the day's stalking be ruined, but an inadequately clad stalker may find himself in real danger from the effects of hypothermia – even in the so-called summer months.

There are three criteria which must be met when choosing clothes for stalking: comfort, safety and concealment. Your garments must keep you relatively warm and dry. If you find yourself lying in a burn with water trickling in at your neck and out by your ankles while a force-nine gale whips sleet flurries into your face, then nothing short of an electrically heated diving suit could provide truly dry warmth. Your clothes should be comfortable to walk and crawl in, not overly close-fitting so that they will restrict free movement. It helps if they can be opened or closed to allow changes in the amount of air which circulates around the body. A long climb up a hill may mean that you need to unbutton your jacket to keep cool, while the wind at the top when you sit down to spy could rapidly chill you unless the buttons are re-fastened.

Boots that cause blisters, badly fitting socks that ruck up under your heels, tight trousers and coats that drag as you walk, waterproofs that act like a turkish bath by trapping perspiration and stiff collars that cut into your neck will all help to spoil the enjoyment of a day on the hill, and all can be avoided with a little forethought.

To a large extent, safety and comfort are interlinked. There are two major dangers to guard against when venturing into the hills – injuries sustained in a fall, and hypothermia as a result of exposure. The best and most experienced climbers can fall, and no one is immune to the effects of cold, wet and fatigue. Part of the attraction of Highland stalking is the element of hardship associated with walking long distances over rough country. When you come home from a long day on the hill, tired, perhaps cold and wet, legs aching with unaccustomed climbing and walking, it is the realisation that you have worked hard for your stag – pushed yourself to your limits in order to conclude a successful stalk – that brings the inner glow of satisfaction when you sink into a hot bath with a glass of

Wet waterproofs can appear almost black when seen at a distance.

something warming in your fist. The stalker does not seek danger in the way that a rock climber does, but the element of danger is there and, for some stalkers at any rate, it may add to the enjoyment of the day.

A good pair of boots, coupled with a sensible appreciation of your own capabilities, is the best protection against a fall, while a stick can also be invaluable for maintaining balance. There is an excellent variety of thermal and waterproof clothing available from outdoor, climbing and camping shops as well as from rod and gun retailers, but unfortunately much of it fails to meet the third criterion for stalking dress – the necessity for concealment.

Climbers, walkers and skiers all face the same problems as the stalker when they venture into the hills – they need to keep warm, dry and generally upright. However, the climber or hiker likes to wear bright colours so that the job of the rescue services is made easier in the event of an accident. Jackets and cagoules in Dayglo orange, red, yellow and blue are excellent for this purpose and can be seen all too clearly at great distances, as many a stalker will know to his cost. There is something peculiarly frustrating about spending half a day creeping and crawling to within range of a stag, only to see it trot away as a party of walkers looms over the horizon. Even the most taciturn of Highlanders may become uncharacteristically eloquent at such moments.

Next to the luminous jackets of climbers and walkers, the colours that show up most clearly on the hills are black and white. It should hardly be necessary to say that no one should consider going stalking in white clothing, except perhaps hind stalking in the snow, but many stalkers do go to the hill in clothes that, from a distance at any rate, appear to be black. Most of the waxed jackets sold, and a great deal of the lightweight waterproof clothing available from field sports retailers, is coloured dark green. Seen close at hand it would appear that such clothing would blend in well on the hill, but from any distance, particularly if it is raining and the clothing is wet, the wearer will appear to be dressed in black.

73

Camouflage pattern clothing is very effective at breaking up the outline of the wearer, especially at close range, though it is less useful at longer distances.

I have often sat and watched a shooting party working their pointers some distance away on the hill. The first thing that catches the eye is usually the dog, especially if it is predominantly white, as many pointers are. Once the dog has attracted your attention the next step is to spy for the shooting party itself, and if one of them is wearing a waxed jacket it is a fair bet that he will be the one you spot. By contrast, some of the quite light fawn or grey/green clothes can be very hard to spot and it is usually movement that gives them away rather than colour. Even the familiar military camouflage-type of coat will look black at any distance over about a quarter of a mile.

The irregular camouflage pattern is designed to break up the outline of the wearer and it is quite effective at doing this at close quarters, in woodland or scrub, for example. At longer distances, however, the eye sees only a dark, upright shape, since the human eye is not keen enough to distinguish the pattern any more and the effect of the camouflage is lost. This is not to deny the efficacy of such patterns at closer ranges – when crawling on an exposed face, for example – when the broken-up outline is probably of real value. At long distances, the hill assumes a kind of pattern, and the eye is drawn to anything that interrupts it. Movement will always attract the eye, as will anything that seems out of place in the general scheme of things. Any dark, upright shape will catch the human eye and presumably have the same effect on deer.

As well as the colour of stalking clothes, we must also consider noise when thinking about concealment. Some types of waterproof can be very noisy when

Hind stalking in winter. No matter what clothing is worn, stalking in these conditions is hard, freezing work.

rubbing against heather or rock, or when the legs rub against each other while walking. It may not be noticeable on a windy day, but it can seem horribly loud when the wind is still. If you can hear it, so can the deer. It won't matter when you are half a mile away, but if you are crawling towards a beast which is only fifty yards ahead then the slightest whisper is enough to catch its attention. Test before you buy by rubbing the cloth against itself. If it sounds too loud, look for an alternative.

The same rules obviously apply to clothing as to equipment: you have to take everything you need with you as there is no going back for an extra pullover or pair of gloves once you are on the hill. As with the other equipment, weight and bulk will be important factors in deciding what is, and what is not, acceptable as stalking wear. You are either going to be wearing or carrying every item of clothing that you take, and we have already seen that bulky, hiker-type rucksacks are not suitable for stalkers. A coat carried over the arm will seem to weigh far more than the same coat when it is being worn and it will be a nuisance when you try to use your binoculars.

The time of year will obviously have an influence on the amount of gear that you take to the hill with you. An unexpected change in the weather in August may be very unpleasant if you have left your waterproofs behind but the same situation in January might have far more serious consequences. If you are uncertain, it is always advisable to err on the side of caution. Very few stalkers succumb to heat-stroke in the Highlands but hypothermia is an ever-present possibility. Let us consider the type of outfit that should be suitable for most stalking areas, starting at the feet and working our way upwards.

BOOTS

The best boot for stalking will depend, to a great extent, on where and when you are going. One forest may be predominantly steep, rocky ground, another might be wet, boggy flow country. The summer stalker will be concerned with grip, ankle protection and keeping his feet dry; the stalker who goes after hinds in January or February must add insulation to those requirements. Wet feet in summer and autumn are uncomfortable; wet feet in winter may mean the onset of a bout of frostbite.

Wellingtons are definitely not to be recommended, except perhaps where the ground is entirely flat and boggy. They generally lack sufficient grip on their soles, give little support to the ankles and are hot and uncomfortable to walk in for any distance. Having said that, I know of at least one professional stalker who wears them regularly, and not on a flat piece of ground by any standards. They will serve at a pinch, but any good walking boot, or even shoe, will probably be better.

Some stalkers prefer a stout shoe to boots, particularly for summer wear. Shoes are lighter and therefore less tiring than boots and better ventilated in warm weather. On the other hand, they have the dual disadvantages of offering no support for the ankles and having a considerably lower waterline than a boot. If you decide on boots rather than shoes there are three principal types of material open to you. The traditional leather boot, waterproof rubber ankle boots and the more recently introduced lightweight boots, with uppers of leather and nylon, rather in the fashion of a running shoe.

Boots for the hill. The stalker, on the left, is wearing rubber soled Bridgedale Dryboots; the Rifle favours the more traditional nailed boot in leather.

Leather boots are probably the first choice for the majority of stalkers. A good leather boot will last for many years and, because leather allows the feet to breathe, will keep the wearer's feet dry and comfortable when those in a rubber boot would have become soaked with perspiration. Leather is very resistant to scrapes and scratches from rocks and stone which are common on the hill and, having a certain amount of natural give will, in time, mould itself to the shape of your feet.

By the same token, leather boots need a quite considerable spell of breaking in before they can be worn for long periods, or to walk long distances, and this should be done well before arriving in Scotland for your stalking holiday. A good, long walk in brand new boots on the first day out could mean that there would be no further stalking for the rest of the week while you waited for the blisters to heal. Leather boots also need a certain amount of regular maintenance to keep them supple and water resistant.

Dubbin, boot polish, and various oils and waxes are the traditional methods of treating boots, with the more recent addition of silicone sprays and dips which are supposed to make the leather completely waterproof. The problem on many Highland hills is not just the wet – which all the different treatments will handle with varying degrees of success – but the friction of the boot, particularly the toe-caps, against the grass and heather. A mile or two through wet heather will rub away practically any treatment and the boot will then slowly absorb water through the bare leather.

Rubber boots stop water coming in from the outside, but they also trap perspiration on the inside, besides which, if any water is shipped over the tops of the boots it is in there for the day, or until you stop and remove the boots to bail out. The Bridgedale Dryboot has become extremely popular (at least in this area), in the past few years, being a rubber ankle boot lined with a soft, absorbent material which is both warm and comfortable in use. They have several advantages and one or two disadvantages compared with leather boots. On the plus side, they are waterproof, warm and very comfortable to wear without the need for any breaking-in period, as well as being considerably cheaper than a good leather boot. However, they have an unfortunate tendency to split along the seams below the lacing eyes, and the eyes themselves sometimes pull out when tightening the laces. Though their grip is excellent when new, the soft rubber sole wears away much faster than a Vibram or Commando sole, and once most of the tread has worn they are absolutely lethal on snow or ice. That said, and bearing their price in mind, they are an excellent choice, especially for the stalker who will only be going to the hill a few times each year.

The modern nylon-and-leather-topped boots can be fine for summer use, being lightweight, well ventilated and with good quality soles for grip. They are not designed to be waterproof and will, of course, let out the water as readily as they let it in. Weighing less than a traditional leather shoe, but still providing ankle support, they are a useful and slightly cheaper alternative to leather, though obviously not designed for use in the hills during winter.

Whatever your choice of uppers, it is essential that the soles of your boots provide you with a firm grip. There are two basic choices of sole: leather soles

On this occasion, the stalker is wearing ordinary rubber boots for stalking in boggy peat hags.

studded with nails, and rubber composition soles such as the Vibram and Commando ones already mentioned. Nailed boots have a strong following among those people who work in the hills all the year round, such as shepherds, gamekeepers, farmers and professional stalkers, while the composition soles, particularly the Vibrams, are the usual choice of serious hill walkers. Nailed boots will grip on steep, grassy slopes where a composition sole may be less effective, but conversely, a nailed boot is very noisy on rocky ground which a rubber sole would cross silently.

If you are buying new boots for stalking beware of buying the very heavy, and very expensive, mountain boots, sold for use in alpine climbing. If you already own such a pair of boots and intend to use them for stalking, then there is no reason why you cannot, but in general they are too stiff and heavy for the kind of walking that you are likely to be doing, as well as being unnecessarily expensive.

SOCKS

The best boots in the world will not be comfortable if they are worn over ill-fitting socks. Wool is undoubtedly the best material to choose. It stays warm even when wet and, being less harsh than most man-made fibres, is less likely to cause blisters. Choose socks with a good thick foot, since this will provide additional cushioning to the soles of your feet and add greatly to your comfort when walking. If your boots are large enough to allow, you may choose to wear two pairs of socks. Provided the inner pair does not ruck up under your instep, the extra thickness will add to both warmth and comfort.

A common arrangement is to wear a pair of knee-length stockings underneath and a shorter pair of socks on top. The long stockings are fastened with ties or garters where they meet the legs of breeches or plus-fours and the short, outer socks are turned down over the cuffs of boots. They will thus help to prevent stones or bits of heather getting inside the boots and causing irritation. Beware of reversing the arrangement and putting the short socks on to your feet first; they will almost inevitably slide down during the day, and then boots and outer socks will have to be removed in order to straighten them.

Your feet can come in for a lot of unaccustomed punishment in the course of a day's stalking. Clean, well fitting socks will go a long way to minimising any damage and help to prevent your stalking being spoiled.

BREEKS

Some form of knee-length garment – breeches, plus-twos or plus-fours – is the usual choice of the stalker in preference to full-length trousers. Breeks (I will use this word to include all varieties of knee-length trouser), allow greater freedom of movement to the legs, don't flap around in the wind and don't get wet and cling to your legs in the way that trousers do. If your legs get soaked with rain, or from walking through long, wet vegetation, trousers will remain soggy and uncomfortable for hours, perhaps even for the rest of the day. In contrast, a pair of woollen socks will dry out relatively quickly and, in any case, have the property of remaining warm even when wet.

If you are walking through peat hags it is inevitable that a certain amount of peat will get transferred from the heels of your boots on to your legs. A muddied pair of socks can be rinsed out and, if there is a decent drying room available, be ready for wear the next day. Even if there are no drying facilities, it is much easier and cheaper to pack a couple of extra pairs of socks than to bring a spare pair of trousers for use on the hill. In one respect, though, trousers do score over breeks. They will help to keep the midges out of your socks and on occasion this might far outweigh all their other disadvantages. In general, however, breeks, coupled with a good spray of insect repellent will be the best choice for the stalker.

The choice between breeks, plus-twos and plus-fours is one for the individual. It is not advisable to buy breeks which are only just long enough to fasten below the knee since they will inevitably part company with the tops of your socks at every opportunity. Baggy knees may not look very smart and fashionable when you try them on in the shop, but they will allow much greater freedom of movement when walking or crawling. Belt loops are useful. A belt helps to keep your shirt tucked in, and in any case, you may need a belt to fasten your knife on. Good, deep pockets lessen the chance of anything you put in them being lost when crawling and button-down flaps give added security. Loose breeks are to be preferred to tight-fitting ones. Freedom of movement has already been mentioned and there are the added advantages of being able to add extra layers of underclothes in cold weather with a lessening of strain on the seams. A split pair of breeks will provide a lot of fun for everyone, except the unfortunate who is wearing them at the time. You may well laugh about it afterwards (especially if you were a spectator, not the main participant), but it will be cold and wet at the time, not to mention what havoc the midges might wreak.

Breeks are made in a variety of materials, but the best choice for the stalker is undoubtedly a good quality, heavy-weight tweed. Tweed is warm, even when wet (provided it is proper woollen tweed), tough, hard-wearing and silent in use. There is a wide variety of colours and patterns on sale, many designed specifically for use by stalkers. Other materials, particularly the denim used to make jeans, become cold and clammy at the first shower of rain and lose all their insulating properties.

Unfortunately, tweed of the best quality is not a cheap material. A pair of tweed breeks may cost twice the price of a similar garment in moleskin, corduroy or a man-made tweed substitute. If you can afford the price, then good tweed is excellent value for money and should give many years of service. Tweeds made of a mixture of wool and man-made fibres are the next best thing, and while costing a good deal less will lose some of the properties of insulation and toughness of all-wool material. Loden cloth is claimed to have many of the properties of good tweed, being hard-wearing and practically waterproof, but there is little difference in price between the two materials.

Corduroy and moleskin are both adequate, though neither will keep you as warm and dry as tweed. Moleskin is very tough-wearing but tends to absorb a lot of water and can weigh very heavily at the end of a long rainy day. It also becomes almost white after repeated washing and will tend to make the wearer unnecessarily conspicuous.

If you are on a very tight budget then a pair of ex-army khaki trousers – the heavy, rough kind, not parade-ground style – make an acceptable alternative. They can be worn tucked into your socks, or converted to breeches by a simple operation involving only a pair of scissors. Leave plenty of material below the knee if you do this – it is easier to cut off a bit more than it is to sew some back on. If you want to make a really good job of them, a proper seam, a short tuck in the sides, and a button or a bit of velcro will turn them into a passable pair of breeks; if not, then two quick slashes with the scissors will work nearly as well in practice. The bits you cut off the legs can be sewn on to the knees as reinforcement. Double knees and seats are well worth having in breeks for the hill. The double seat helps keep you dry when sitting down and double knees can greatly extend the life of the garment, especially if you do a lot of crawling through rough and stony ground.

JACKETS

As far as the material for a jacket goes, simply re-read what was written about breeks. Tweed is the traditional choice, and as far as I know there is nothing to better it. All the same reasons apply: silent, inconspicuous, warm when wet,

Camouflage jacket for the stalker, tweed for the Rifle, as they watch a stag away over the horizon.

almost waterproof and very hard-wearing. It is also very expensive, and the thought of spending £100 or more on a jacket and then crawling through a peat hag in it may be too much to bear, particularly for the occasional stalker.

Fortunately, there are no rules to say that you need a new, or a smart jacket to wear to the hill. A jumble sale, or your local Oxfam shop could well yield a cast-off treasure that would be perfect for stalking. It doesn't even have to fit particularly well, though too big is obviously better than too small, since it will allow easy movement and leave space for plenty of layers underneath in cold weather. Lighter colours are to be preferred to darker ones, but either will do. Don't be tempted by one of the very lightweight and loosely woven jackets sold as fashionable tweed garments. They let the rain through very quickly and are designed more for everyday wear than for protection from the weather. Plenty of good, deep pockets, preferably with button-down flaps, are useful, and lapels that will button across the throat and keep the rain out of your neck can be a real blessing at times. A proper suit with matching trousers and jacket looks very smart, but the odds are that the trousers will have worn out long before the jacket does.

COATS AND LEGGINGS

There is rather a fine line to be drawn somewhere between a coat and a jacket. To some extent the terms are interchangeable, particularly with regard to the waxed-cotton jackets (coats?) so popular among field sportsmen everywhere. For the purposes of this chapter I am thinking of a jacket as a garment which is partially wind and weather proof, but which will probably be replaced by, or covered over with, a coat on the wettest and coldest days.

The stalker has two possible alternatives when choosing waterproof outer garments. (Actually there are three. One stalker friend claims never to have worn a waterproof on the hill. When asked what he did when it rained he replied, simply and obviously, 'I get wet'.) The tweed jacket can be replaced by a waxed-cotton coat, or perhaps one made from one of the more modern fibres such as Goretex, which serves the same purpose as a jacket while being heavier, warmer and more wind and water proof. In very cold weather, the outer coat might be worn over the tweed jacket (at other times it would be chosen in its stead). The other alternative is to keep wearing the tweed jacket, but to slip a set of the very lightweight proofed nylon waterproofs into one of the pockets. These would be put on and removed as the weather dictated, and are so light that they will be almost unnoticed in a jacket pocket.

Waxed coats are very, very tough, almost completely waterproof if waxed regularly, and will allow a certain amount of perspiration to escape through their fibres. On the other hand they are heavy, can be rather too warm at times and are too bulky to carry in comfort. We have already seen that they may be overly conspicuous, especially when wet, and they are noticeably noisier than tweed when walking or brushing against rock or heather. They will last a long time and can be repaired when the inevitable rips and tears damage them.

In weather like this, a good coat, hat and leggings are essential, and you will still be frozen stiff at the end of the day.

The lightweight waterproofs such as those in the Peter Storm range make a good alternative to a full-weight coat. They can be carried in the pockets and only put on as needed, then, once a shower has passed will dry out in a few minutes ready to go back in the pocket. A pair of leggings plus a hooded jacket will cover you almost completely, leaving just face, hands and boot toes exposed to the weather. They are also useful to slip on over your coat and breeks when the time comes to crawl in to a stag; especially welcome if the crawl promises to be a wet and peaty one. They are almost completely windproof and waterproof and will keep in the warmth provided by the layers of clothes beneath them. Almost inevitably, however, there is a minus side to consider as well.

Like the waxed coats, they are sometimes noisy, and will appear almost as dark as waxed cotton when wet. They are far less robust and much harder to mend if they get ripped. A small hole will very rapidly become a large hole with only the slightest encouragement. They can be quite dangerous on snowy or wet, grassy slopes, since, should you fall they will act like a toboggan – an exhilarating experience provided the slope doesn't end in a precipice. Obviously, they are considerably cheaper than waxed coats, but they cannot be expected to last nearly as long. Since the fabric is almost completely waterproof, not only will it stop rain coming in from the outside, it will also stop perspiration escaping from within. On a warm day particularly, the wearer may find he is just as wet inside his nylon garments as if he had simply let the rain pour down on to himself. This is a fault with practically all waterproofs, though some brands are much worse than others. It is a problem, even in cold weather, since the body still perspires, even if less visibly and a damp layer of clothing next to the skin will have a definite cooling effect despite the protection of outer layers.

There are some fabrics available now which claim to be both waterproof and properly ventilated, such as Goretex and Ventile. If they are really as good as is claimed they will be a real boon to the hill stalker, but as yet they are very expensive, and the one Goretex coat of which I have personal experience rattled like a kettle drum during a shower of rain.

Everything I have said about coats will apply equally to leggings. When choosing a pair of waterproof leggings do make sure that the ends of the legs are wide enough to pull on over your boots. You won't want to stop and remove boots every time you decide to put on or remove leggings. I prefer the trouser-type leggings to the ones which clip to the belt and just cover the legs as it is possible to sit down in comfort when wearing the former. It helps if there are slits to allow access to your breeks pockets, and they should be long enough to reach beyond the tops of your boots, otherwise they will decant all the water neatly down inside them and on to your feet.

As to size, it is better to err on the generous side since this will allow more layers to be worn underneath when required. Coat zippers which open from top and bottom are useful to allow a varying amount of ventilation. The hood should be big enough to wear over your hat or cap and a good, big toggle on the zipper is easier to grip when your fingers are frozen. Beware of the waxed-cotton coats which are being sold as fashion garments for trendy young things about town. They cost about four times the price of the real thing and will probably be of lower quality. Save your money for something more practical.

HATS

Some kind of hat is almost an essential when stalking. A lot of heat is lost through the top of the head if it is left bare. The hat should have a peak or brim to shield the face, since a bare, white forehead will stick out like the proverbial sore thumb. The colour should be some muted shade that will blend with the colours of the hill. When you have crawled to within range of your beast and you cautiously raise your head to get a look at it, it is your hat that will surface first, so bright, eye-catching shades are definitely out.

The most common hats are deerstalkers, flat caps, or ghillie-style hats, usually in the same shades of tweed as are used for jackets. The deerstalker may look a little archaic, with its connotations of Sherlock Holmes, but it is actually a very practical garment. The twin peaks will keep the rain out of your face and off your neck, and the ear flaps can be tied under the chin in a high wind, keeping the hat firmly anchored to the head as well as warming the ears. Flat caps fit better under a hood and are less liable to tip forward over the eyes when you are taking the shot. As long as you have some sort of hat, in a suitably muted colour, you will be adequately topped out for the hill.

A sheltered spot by the lochside in January. Conditions on the open hill will be far worse.

GLOVES

I am told that the old stalkers used to hold their hands under the ice in a burn for a few minutes at the start of a cold day on the hill. With the circulation thus stimulated they never needed to wear gloves. It is probably true, and I pass on the idea for what it is worth. For myself, and other less hardy souls, gloves are the answer to cold hands.

Any glove that keeps your hands warm and dry will do. There are some very comfortable-looking gloves on offer in the ski shops, but most of them are too brightly coloured, and perhaps too expensive, for the stalker. The real test of a glove comes when you have to start crawling, and any that are not completely waterproof will soon be saturated. You can always put them in a pocket until the crawl is over, then use them to re-heat your hands, though this may mean taking the shot with numbed and frozen fingers. A good, and cheap combination is a pair of woollen gloves worn under waxed-cotton mittens. Provided you keep plenty of wax on them (just rub a dollop of proofing wax around while wearing them), they are both warm and waterproof and can be quickly slipped off when it is time to take the shot.

ODDS AND ENDS

A pair of canvas, or proofed-nylon, gaiters can be very useful. They will help keep your boots and socks dry when walking through long heather or grass, and will prevent those annoying little bits of heather stem from creeping down inside your boots. They also keep a lot of the peat and mud off your legs and will allow you to cross quite deep burns dry shod – provided you move quickly enough. Canvas gaiters are heavier than nylon, but allow your legs to breathe – more important in summer than in winter, of course.

A scarf or a length of towelling worn around the neck in wet weather will keep the water off your collar as well as helping to trap heat inside your clothes. What you wear under your stalking outfit is a matter of common sense and personal preference, and will obviously depend on the time of year, the weather forecast and what you have available. In winter, a good set of thermal underwear really does make a tremendous difference to how warm you are, but it will, hopefully, not be needed at other times of the year.

Whatever you wear, you must be willing to crawl through peat hags and lay in a burn with it, if necessary, and not worry unduly if it gets plastered with mud, blood or worse. If you are contemplating having a go at stalking for the first time, then there is probably no need to spend a small fortune on a special outfit; there will always be time for that later if you decide to stalk regularly.

6
Transport on the Hill

On seeing the title of this chapter, the complete novice to stalking might be excused from asking 'What transport?' I have, after all, just spent the better part of the previous chapter discussing footwear, with much emphasis on the distances that the Highland stalker may have to walk in pursuit of his sport. The answer, of course, is that the transport is not required, at least not primarily, in order to convey the stalking party around in ease and comparative comfort. Human feet are perfectly adequate for the actual approach and stalk; transport only becomes essential when the results of a successful stalk have to be taken home to the deer larder.

A Highland stag will weigh somewhere in the region of fourteen stone after he has been gralloched. A very good stag might weigh in excess of twenty stone, and hinds, though considerably smaller than stags, will weigh between nine and twelve stone. No matter what the weight, once a beast has been stalked and shot it has to be taken back to the larder ready to be butchered, or collected by the game dealer. You may feel up to the challenge of carrying fourteen stone of raw venison over ten miles of rough country and if you do, then you're a better man than I am. Start walking while the rest of us consider the alternatives. We'll catch you up later.

There are times when it is necessary to use nothing but muscle power to move a beast, though the usual arrangement would be to drag rather than carry it. There may be places on the forest where no pony, wheeled or tracked vehicle can reach, and if a stag or hind is shot in one of these places then dragging may be the only practical way to get it out.

It is quite possible to drag a stag by his antlers, or a hind by her front legs, but the task is made a lot simpler if a length of rope is to hand. The rope is fastened to the base of the antlers of the stag, with a loop caught round the end of the nose to stop the lower jaw digging in to the ground. If there are two of you to drag, then the rope can be fixed at its mid-point with one end leading to each dragger. Take a hold, pull, and keep on pulling until you get to where you want to go. If you are carrying a stick, the end of the rope can be fastened to the stick and the stag pulled with a grip on the shaft of the stick – much easier on the hands than heaving on a thin rope. Alternatively, a single rope can be fastened to the middle of the stick and one man can grasp on either side of the rope.

How difficult the task will be will depend partly on the size of the beast you have to drag, but much more on the nature of the ground you have to cross. A drag down a smooth, gentle slope is a comparatively easy affair. A quite gentle pressure on the rope will keep the beast moving along behind, and you may

Dragging a stag – not too difficult when going down hill.

wonder what the objection is to moving your victim by muscle power alone. Just wait until you try to drag a beast up a slope, or worse, through broken, rocky ground. Going uphill, the problem is obviously gravity – the same force that made life so simple when you were going down. The steeper the slope, the harder it is to make progress, though strangely enough the situation does not work in reverse.

A very steep downhill drag is not as easy as might appear at first sight. Gravity helps, but at times it tries to help too much, and instead of you dragging the stag, it can start to drag you. Fourteen stone of dead stag with a set of very sharp antlers as a figure-head is a quite lethal projectile once it gets out of control, and you will be somewhere in its direct line of travel. Resist the temptation to perform any heroics, step smartly aside and comfort yourself in the knowledge that the beast is probably headed in the right general direction anyway. You can always catch up later.

Broken, rocky ground makes for difficult dragging as well, since hooves, antlers, legs and jaws will all wedge behind boulders and in crevices at every possible opportunity. It is hard, hot, sweaty work and always engenders the greatest admiration in my mind for those old-time stalkers who regularly dragged carcases for long distances as a matter of course. There are some deer forests where dragging is the only practical way, short of a helicopter, of getting beasts off the hill. Fortunately, such places are in a minority and generally there is some easier way to bring deer home to the larder. The traditional method, which is still used on many forests, is to load the beast on to the back of a pony and carry it home like that.

Until quite recently the hill pony, or garron, was the accepted way of fetching stags and hinds home from the hill. Deer forests were the last places in Britain where working horses were kept, and used, because they were the best, and sometimes the only, way to accomplish a task. There are still some dray horses and farm horses at work around the country, but they are being worked because someone, probably from a love of horses or of tradition, chooses to stick to the old ways despite the 'advances' of the twentieth century. In contrast, deer were still being brought home on the backs of ponies because there was simply no alternative.

While there is no such place as a typical Highland deer forest – the terrain varying in some degree wherever you go – it is true to say that much, if not most, of the land used for stalking is inaccessible to all normal forms of transport. A great deal of the Highlands is, just as the name suggests, mountainous – steep and rocky ground, cut through with burns and gullies and littered with huge boulders. Steep slopes may be covered with loose scree, there are moraines dumped by the glaciers at the end of the last ice age, and sudden, vertical faces where some ancient fault line has caused a break in the underlying rock. Even on comparatively level areas there may be boggy pools and deep peat hags. The vegetation overlying the peat is often quite fragile and a heavy vehicle will quickly break through the heather into the peat beneath, sinking inexorably up to its axles. Little wonder that horses were needed to bring the venison off the hill. Even the sure-footed garrons had to take care where they were walking.

A number of alternatives to horse power have become common in the Highlands during the past few years, but many forests still stick to the traditional way of bringing home their beasts. Sometimes this is for reasons of sentiment, but often the pony is kept working because it is still the best way to get the job done. The modern all-terrain vehicle has an amazing ability to cross country but there are still some forests where nothing but a pony can get to certain parts of the ground. In these places, and I suspect in many others, the hill pony will be a familiar sight for many years to come.

Leaving aside the nature of the terrain, there are certain advantages and disadvantages to pony power. To begin with, a pony has to be fed, all the year round, whether it is working or not. It has to be shod, stabled, treated by the vet when sick and generally looked after. The actual cost of keeping a pony will depend on the amount of fodder that has to be bought in from outside the estate. If there is a farm producing a hay crop, then winter keep will be much more economical than if it has to be purchased from elsewhere.

Mechanical transport also has to be fed with petrol or diesel oil, but only for as long as it is in use. When not required, it can be stabled in the garage and need cost nothing until it is needed again – nothing except depreciation which can be quite a heavy burden. If it is mechanical it can break, and if it can break it will, so there are almost certainly going to be repair and maintenance costs with any form of motor vehicle. A pony can have a working life of around twenty years – far longer than any of the all-terrain vehicles (ATVs) currently available. A single pony should outlast four or five mechanical horses – not all that surprising when you consider the kind of terrain they are going to be working over. And the ATV has not yet been invented that can reproduce itself; the pony can provide you with a foal to take its place.

The most common form of transport on the hill. Stalker and Rifle using the cover of a burn to walk out at the start of the day.

Faced with the above, it may seem surprising that the ATV has managed to gain a foothold in the Highlands at all. However, there are one or two ways in which it can outperform four-legged transport and one final, overriding reason why the horse has been replaced on many, many deer forests.

A pony can only carry a single stag, or two hinds, at a time while most of the ATVs will cope quite happily with three or four stags or perhaps half a dozen hinds and carry the stalking party into the bargain. Some of the lighter vehicles can cross boggy flow ground that would be too soft for a pony, and can provide the stalker with year round transport for himself and his dogs, when heather burning perhaps, or visiting fox dens in spring time. They are generally faster than a pony, have lights for use after dark and may be equipped with hoods and heaters to insulate the operator from the worst of the weather. There are disadvantages and advantages to ATVs, just as there are for ponies, but one reason above all others has contributed to the fall in the number of working garrons. The pony must have a ponyman and his wages will far outweigh the cost of most of the alternatives.

If a pony is to be used to fetch home a stag or hind the pony and ponyman will accompany the stalker and Rifle as they set out for the hill. Somewhere along the way, before the stalk has begun in earnest, pony and ponyman will wait behind while the stalking party go on in pursuit of their quarry. Then, once the stalk has been satisfactorily concluded, the pony will be brought up to where its cargo is waiting, the beast will be loaded, and pony, handler and stag will start their journey back home. In contrast, if a mechanical vehicle is to be used there is no need for the extra man. Stalker and Rifle can ride out to the hill in the vehicle, leave it somewhere while they are stalking, then return for it once they have a beast to be loaded. If it is early in the day and further beasts are to be culled, they can leave the vehicle again and start another stalk. One man's wages are saved, and that must be an important consideration in today's financial climate.

It may seem unlikely, but some forests have changed from ponies to mechanical transport, not because of the cost of a ponyman, but because it has proved impossible to find anyone willing and capable of taking on the job. A hill pony may not always be the most co-operative of animals – my dictionary defines 'garron' as 'a small inferior horse bred in Ireland and Scotland', but I wouldn't like to be the one to call a hill pony 'inferior'. They can be stubborn brutes, especially when going away from home and, like all working horses, need a certain amount of looking after, though they are tough and hardy, as any animal must be which winters in the Highlands.

A ponyman's job can be very agreeable in good weather, but it must be a cold and lonely business to spend a long day sitting in the rain waiting for the signal to move up and join a stalking party. Signalling today may well be done by means of a two-way radio; in the past the normal method of calling up the pony, if out of direct line of sight, was to light a little fire of heather and send a smoke signal. This could be difficult at times, especially when everything on the hill was soaking wet, but there were other days when a fire was easily started. One local man lit a twist of heather on a fine, dry and breezy day, the wind caught hold of the flames and, by the time the fire was finally stopped, 14,000 acres had gone up in smoke. In practice, a much smaller fire than this is usually enough to catch the ponyman's attention.

There is something that seems right about a hill pony trudging steadily back towards the deer larder with a stag bumping gently in the saddle. Hill ponies are often real characters in their own right – old friends to the guests who see them year after year. They are quiet, ecologically sound, cause minimal disturbance on the hill and form a romantic link with the deerstalkers of the past. They do very little damage to the flora of the Highlands. They may eat some of it, but they don't crush it down and make ugly, black, peaty tracks across the hill as so many vehicles do. Many of those who come to the Highlands to stalk will mourn the passing of the hill pony though I suspect that some professional stalkers will take a less sentimental view, especially when they are hind stalking on their own during the winter.

Many deer forests have stables dotted about on their further out beats. Often in the loneliest, wildest parts of the ground, miles from the nearest human habitation, they are bleak and forsaken, even when seen in the warmth of a summer's morning. In times past, ponymen would have been stationed in these stables, living there with no company but their horses from July until November. I wonder if they would mourn the hill pony, or welcome the arrival of the internal combustion engine on the hill?

There is quite a variety of vehicles on sale at the time of writing, all designed to cope with the hills and moors of stalking country. There are two main problems for the designer to solve: they must have enough power and traction to cope with steep hills while still being stable enough to use in safety, and they

Spying for deer from an Argocat – typical of the modern all-terrain vehicles used for stalking.

must exert a low enough ground pressure to avoid breaking through the upper layers of vegetation above the peat and becoming bogged. The designers' solution, in most cases, has been to build a lightweight vehicle with a low centre of gravity, thus minimising power requirements and enhancing stability. There are two general solutions to the problem of breaking through the surface and bogging – ATVs usually running on tracks like a tank, or on big, balloon tyres.

A notable exception to the general run of lightweight, low ground pressure vehicles is the Snow-trac. This, as its name implies, was designed with arctic conditions in mind, and is a very powerful, heavy and expensive, tracked vehicle. Obviously excellent in winter, it is also very mobile across hill and moor, but there is one major snag. If you do succeed in bogging a Snow-trac out in some remote corner away from the road, then nothing except another Snow-trac is going to be mobile enough to reach it and powerful enough, to un-bog it. It is possible to shift most of the other vehicles by human muscle alone, aided perhaps by some sort of lever.

The most common of the smaller vehicles used by stalkers is the Argocat, but there are several other designs on the market such as the VeePee, the Garron and the Transcraft. Some run on tracks, the others on balloon tyres, and there is sometimes an option to fit tracks over tyres for use in soft snow. Since the Argocat is the most common, as well as being fairly typical of the breed, I will describe it in more detail. However, much of the following will apply equally to the other makes of all-terrain vehicles.

The Argo has a plastic body shell, rather reminiscent of a square bath tub in

Harsh conditions during a Highland winter as the stalker spies a distant bunch of deer from a snow-crusted Argo.

design, mounted on a steel chassis. An engine of about seventeen horsepower is mounted in front and drives all the wheels (six or eight according to model) through a split clutch and a two speed gearbox. The drive is transmitted to the wheels by means of chains and the vehicle is steered by two brake levers, each acting on one bank of wheels. A hand throttle controls speed, and this, plus the gear selection lever and the steering brakes are the only controls, apart from light switches and windscreen wipers, if fitted. Steering is done by braking the wheels on one side of the machine while the other set of wheels continues to drive, thus slewing the Argo around in the manner of a tank. Top speed is in the region of fifteen miles per hour on a good surface; in practice the type of ground will govern the speed at which it is safe, and comfortable, to travel.

Two people can sit in relative comfort in the front and extra seats can be fitted to allow four more to sit in the back. There are various other additions which add to the degree of luxury enjoyed by the occupants – windscreens, canvas covers, side windows and so on. There is no suspension other than that afforded by the cushioning of the tyres, and an Argo can be a real boneshaker, particularly over rough ground. It is a very stable vehicle, will climb and descend quite hair-raising gradients, drag its way through bogs and pools, cross lochs and rivers – the tyres will keep it afloat even if punctured – and can even be fitted with an outboard motor. It is almost, but not quite, impossible to turn one over, and most drivers will have decided to err on the side of discretion long before the limits of its stability are reached.

Steering is simple – just pull on the brake lever on the side to which you wish to turn – but it takes a lot of practice before the beginner can drive smoothly. At first there is a tendency to snatch at the brakes or ease back on the throttle when cornering, resulting in erratic and jerky progress. Once the technique is mastered though, an Argo can be driven in a relatively stately fashion and,

Not just useful for stalking. An ATV being used here to take a shooting party out to the hill.

provided that the ground is not too rough, can convey its passengers in something akin to comfort. If fitted with a canvas hood it will keep the worst of the weather off its occupants, and a certain amount of heat from the engine and brakes finds its way through to the front seat passengers.

Noise is inevitable from any vehicle which is propelled by a petrol engine and one of the charges frequently laid against Argocats and the like is that they cause unnecessary disturbance on the hill. It can become quite an emotive issue among stalkers, some insisting that the sound of an Argo will put every beast for miles into precipitate flight, while the opposite camp will say that it is possible to drive to within a few hundred yards of deer without alarming them unduly.

In my opinion, it is not the noise itself that is the culprit. Our home is below the flightline of one of the RAF low level training areas and, at times jet aircraft pass only a few feet above our heads. The noise is indescribable, but feeding deer will not even raise their heads. They are used to the sound, do not associate it with danger, and have learned to ignore it. They will sometimes act in the same way when an Argo is passing – a casual glance, then back to grazing or chewing their cud. Indeed, during the worst of the winter weather, our Argocat is used to cart hay out to the hinds and they will run right up to it to get their daily rations. However, those same hinds may take flight at the merest hint of an Argo engine on other occasions, particularly if the Argo is carrying a stalking party. Why, I don't know, but I would guess that the animals get used to seeing and hearing a vehicle in a particular place and learn that it represents no threat under those circumstances. If the same vehicle appears where it is not customarily seen then natural caution overrides their conditioned acceptance of the vehicle under 'normal' circumstances, and they react to it as a threat.

The distance from which an engine can be heard will vary tremendously according to the terrain and the prevailing weather conditions. Given a still, quiet day I can sometimes hear an Argo over the full length of our loch – a fraction over three miles. If there is a strong or gusty wind, then that same vehicle may be completely undetectable to my ears at a couple of hundred yards.

Hinds and calves alerted by the noise of a vehicle, and about to disappear over the ridge.

A deer's hearing is probably at least as acute as a human's, and it is reasonable to assume that they will experience the same variety of distance detection, or perhaps even more. There are certainly times when it is possible to drive very close to deer in an ATV and for them to raise no more signs of alarm than a careful study as you are passing; but this does not mean that the beasts are becoming so accustomed to the vehicle that its presence will eventually be ignored. It is worth considering how often deer have vacated the ground simply because they have heard a vehicle, and have been out of sight before the vehicle reached the area. These, never having been in view of the stalking party, will not be counted as disturbed beasts. Indeed, they may be safely over the march long before their absence can be noted.

It must not be forgotten, of course, that a man, or men, on foot can also cause disturbance. Getting out of the Argo and walking is not going to magically prevent the deer from moving on. When stalking it is normal to proceed so as to cause the minimum of disturbance, but there are other times when a party may be on the hill in full view of the deer – grouse shooting, heather burning, or just hill walking. On such occasions, as when in a vehicle, the reaction of the deer to human disturbance will vary from day to day. There are times when every beast on the hill will take off at high speed as soon as they catch a glimpse of a distant human figure, and there are others when they will tolerate quite a close approach before wandering away. What is it that will cause a quick retreat one day, but only a watching brief the next? I am afraid I cannot tell you. A great pity, since it would be a most useful piece of knowledge for any stalker.

If the effects of noise are open to debate, there is other evidence of the effect of vehicles on the hill which is only too plain to see. Much of the vegetation in the Highlands consists of a thin mat of living plants on top of a deep bed of sterile, wet peat. As long as the plants can maintain their position on top of the acid peat they will thrive, but if they are forced down below the surface of the peat they will quickly succumb, leaving a slimy, black pool in their place. Once damaged in this way, the vegetation may take years to recover. Too often it is possible to chart the progress of vehicles across the hill by a long line of wet, lifeless peat slime. Once this state has occurred any vehicle will have problems in progressing (the bare peat can be extremely slippery), and so a second track is made alongside the original one, and then a third, and so on.

The damage will vary with the type of vegetation, the nature of the underlying peat and the frequency of passage, but it can be quite substantial in places – sufficiently so for the Nature Conservancy Council to consider placing limits on the areas where ATVs may be used. Some forests have an extensive system of pony paths, often built by gangs of labourers, working by muscle power alone for a few pence per day. Where this is so, it does much to limit the damage caused, though even a proper pony path can soon become cut up after a prolonged spell of wet weather. If you are ever stalking on a forest with an extensive hill path network, then spare a thought for the men who built them working long hours with pick and shovel for about one shilling and eight pence per day. And they didn't have an Argocat to ride to and from work in!

Another type of vehicle which is becoming common in the deer forests is the three-, or four-wheeled motor cycle. To be strictly correct I suppose they should be called motor tricycles, or motor quadricycles, but they are generally referred to as 'bikes' – a contradiction in terms, but common usage. Like the Argocat, they are mounted on big, low-pressure balloon tyres, and will cross very soft ground before bogging down, as well as climbing quite steep hills. There are several different makes and models available but in general, the four-wheelers are better than those with three, especially those equipped with four-wheel drive.

There are normally carriers fitted both at the front and the rear, and it would be possible, with care, to fetch a beast home on these, though a trailer or sledge to drag behind would be a more effective and safer solution. They can pull a considerable weight – I use our bike for carting gravel and it will cope quite happily with around half a ton – but are obviously more effective on level, smooth ground than on boggy, broken or hilly terrain. A four-wheeled trailer equipped with balloon tyres will go almost anywhere the bike can go; two-wheeled trailers are more likely to stick when crossing drains or gullies.

They are considerably quicker on the flat than the Argo type of ATV, but are also less stable. It is quite easy to tip a bike over, whereas an Argo requires real dedication before it will roll. They have a more limited range than an Argo. An experienced motor cycle trials rider could probably prove that statement false, but in practice common sense, or panic, will stop the bike rider while the Argo driver is still quite happily pressing onwards and upwards. They are also much more limited in their carrying capacity, driver and one passenger on the pillion being the sensible limit.

Another type of all-terrain vehicle, the four-wheeled motor cycle being used here to drag a boat out for laying up over winter.

One other form of transport which deserves a mention is boats. If the forest has a loch running through it, then it may well be possible to fetch beasts home to the larder in some sort of boat. An ordinary rowing boat of fourteen feet or more will accommodate a stag, plus stalker and Rifle, but will demand a certain amount of care when loading, particularly if there is no proper jetty to assist. A more sophisticated arrangement in use on one estate involves transporting not only the deer but also the Argocat, which is loaded on to a specially built craft by means of a loading ramp. It is a very satisfactory arrangement, especially on a cold evening, and, at thirty knots, will bring the stalking party home in a far shorter time than any pony or ATV yet invented.

Apart from damage and disturbance, one charge frequently levelled at hill vehicles is that they make stalking too easy by cutting out most of the walking. In the old days, it is said, we had to walk everywhere – out from the lodge in the morning and back home at night. Certainly there was a lot more walking years ago, but it was often the estate staff that put in the extra miles rather than the stalking guests. It was not uncommon for the guest to ride to the hill on a pony; sometimes the same animal which would be used to carry the stag home, sometimes a saddle pony kept for that express purpose. The ponyman and professional stalker would still walk, of course. Those were less democratic times.

It is certainly possible to cut out a great deal of walking by using an ATV, but that is neither the reason for their popularity, nor the correct way to utilise them. If a stalker should make a practice of stalking from his ATV and perhaps shooting beasts from the vehicle, then the deer will soon learn to associate the

Boats are also useful for bringing beasts home to the larder. This one can also carry an Argocat.

The bows of the boat hinge open to allow the Argo to be loaded via ramps.

sight and sound of the vehicle with danger, and will act accordingly. This is not to deny that such things happen, they certainly do. But shooting deer by this method is not stalking, any more than netting a pool might be considered a sporting method of fishing.

Despite cries to the contrary, there are times when the use of a vehicle may actually mean extra walking instead of less. A pony can be left behind, then signalled on as the stalking party moves forward; if an Argo is left behind, as it must be when beginning a stalk, then at some stage you will have to retrace your steps to collect it again. This could happen several times in the course of a day, and the party may well have walked further than if there was no vehicle in the first place. It is not often that a lack of walking spoils the day for the Rifle, especially if he should be less than fully fit. Should you feel that you are not suffering enough for your sport then simply tell the stalker that the stalking is too easy. Just those few words should prove a sovereign remedy for the man who finds himself with an excess of energy at the end of a day on the hill.

Used sensibly, the Argocat and its derivatives are capable of enhancing the enjoyment of a day's stalking, while in no way removing the physical challenge that is so much a part of the sport. They will never evoke the same nostalgic memories as the sight of a hill pony trudging its heavy-laden way home to the larder through the October dusk, but there is no doubt that the all-terrain vehicle is here to stay. In any event, the novice stalker will have little if any

The Highland pony, or garron is still used on many deer forests.

A typically strong, sturdy hill pony.

control over the type of transport that is in use when he takes up the sport. This is a matter for the owner, or factor, of the forest and will depend on a number of circumstances, as outlined earlier. If you do find yourself longing for a return to the old ways, just have a care about how you express it. They may return sooner than you had bargained for.

A guest on the estate where I work once had a short, and admittedly easy, day on the hill, killing his stag and being home at the lodge by early afternoon. Circumstances were that a shootable stag was found, and taken, within a comparatively short distance from the Argocat, and since only one stag was required that day, the beast was loaded, and the party returned home without expending a great deal of energy. Over supper that night the guest coined the phrase 'Armchair Stalking'. By morning the stalker had been made aware of this rather catchy little title. Stalker and guest went to the hill together again that morning, but this time they travelled on foot.

Somehow, they failed to find a shootable beast quite so quickly this day. Indeed, by the time they did eventually get to within rifle range of a stag, stalker and guest had walked, and sometimes crawled, about seventeen miles – seventeen rough, cold and steep miles, in the course of which the guest had fallen into a burn. The stag was shot, and then they walked back home, the guest just in time to fall into a hot bath before supper, the stalker to take the Argo and go back to collect the stag. There were no further complaints that week about modern stalking being too easy for a reasonably fit man.

Armchair Stalking was mentioned again, though no longer as a term of mild derision. The guest was so deeply influenced by his experience that he was moved to write a poem about it. It hangs on the gunroom wall to this day –

Armchair Stalking

Just beware, if you should dare,
To call it Armchair Stalking.
You may find you mustn't mind,
Quite a lot of walking.

7

The Stalker

The term 'stalker' can be used generally, to mean anyone who goes to the hill in pursuit of deer, or more specifically, it may refer to the professional stalker who is employed to lead the stalking party. Stalker is also a job title, often further qualified as with 'Head Stalker', 'Under Stalker', 'Second Stalker', or perhaps 'Single-handed Stalker'. In this respect 'Stalker' and 'Gamekeeper' are largely interchangeable terms, in that the holder of the office may be called either (for example), Head Stalker or Head Keeper. If the estate which employs the man is exclusively a deer forest then the term used will almost certainly be Stalker. If though, there are other sporting species – grouse perhaps, or partridge and pheasant – then Keeper is more likely to be the title.

This chapter is devoted to the professional stalker. It can do no more than take a general look at the work and nature of those who adopt this most skilled and demanding of occupations. Stalkers, like any other group of humans, are a complex and diverse assortment; they are all individuals and therefore all are different. Indeed, it might be maintained by those who have dealings with them, that some stalkers are even more individual than are the general run of men. It is my intention neither to praise nor to condemn, simply to tell it as I see it.

A good stalker is a very skilled professional, and will have become so through years of experience. Stalking can only be learnt on the hill, not by studying books, though the written word can certainly be of assistance, particularly with such things as larder work or the maintenance of vehicles and equipment. It takes a great deal of dedication to become a really top-class stalker and the rewards, in financial terms at any rate, are far from high. Stalking can mean working very long hours, often under appalling weather conditions; it can mean getting soaked to the skin for days on end, being eaten alive by midges or freezing half to death in pursuit of the winter hind cull. Despite this, most men take up the profession from choice, despite often having the ability and opportunity to work at some far less demanding and more financially rewarding job. The stalker who guides you on the hill may have far wider talents than are at first apparent. One of the stalkers on a neighbouring estate to my home is the captain of the county rugby team, another has played darts at international level and a third, from a few miles down the strath, is a lay preacher and a piping instructor.

There is far more to the stalker's job than simply choosing a route that will bring you within rifle-range of a beast without being detected. Before you even set out for the hill he will have had to make a decision on which part of the forest should be stalked that day. A deer forest is commonly divided into several different beats, usually an informal and fairly flexible division, but one which

The stalker must decide which beasts are to be culled. Two very different stags – which would you shoot, if either?

allows easy identification of the areas. This is particularly useful if more than one stalking party is to be on the hill at the same time, both from a safety viewpoint and for the chances of success of both parties.

It is not just a simple matter of visiting each beat in rotation. An experienced stalker will know where the deer are most likely to be found under particular conditions of wind and weather, and where deer have been seen over recent days. The direction of the wind can be vitally important both to the success of the day, and of subsequent days. An unwise stalk under certain wind conditions may move all the deer across the march on to a neighbouring forest, and there they may stay until something, or someone, moves them back. Some beats may be impossible to stalk in one wind and almost guaranteed of success in another. Deer are wild animals, and normally unconfined by any sort of boundary fence. As soon as a beast has four feet over the march, he or she becomes the property of the neighbouring forest, so it is natural to try and hold 'your' deer within your own bounds. If deer have to be moved, then it is preferable to move them on to a different part of your own ground. The good stalker will have all this in mind before ever leaving the lodge.

If the forest is still using ponies to bring beasts home from the hill then the stalker will have to ensure that the ponyman is correctly briefed as to what, where and when his duties for the day will be. It is arguable which is the more frustrating – a pony which ambles on to the scene in the middle of a stalk, or one which seems to have vanished from the face of the earth at the conclusion of one – but neither will be popular. In this respect at least, some form of mechanical transport is more reliable in that it will stay where you put it, provided the hill is not too steep. It may not start when you return for it, however . . .

Before actually starting out for the hill, the stalker will ensure that the Rifle is properly equipped. (In this context 'the Rifle' refers to the guest who will accompany the stalker and actually shoot the stag or hind.) He will check that his companion is suitably dressed, has remembered his stick, binoculars, lunch, etc. and will arrange for him to fire one or two shots at the target if it should be his first day out, or first day for some time. The stalker must be satisfied that his guest is both confident and capable with the rifle before he will allow him to use it against a live target. Once this has been done, the stalking party can set out for the hill in earnest.

Once you reach the area that is to be the beat for the day, the first thing to be done is to find out what deer are on the ground. You take your binoculars and search the side of the hill, hopefully locating all the deer that are in sight before deciding which are to be the subjects of the stalk. If you are new to stalking then this is likely to be a first demonstration of the stalker's ability and it can be quite a salutary experience, especially if you thought you had twenty-twenty vision.

Scan the hill with your binoculars and it is quite likely that all you will see is grey rock and green vegetation. Meanwhile listen to the muttered commentary from the man alongside you as he looks at the same hill through his own binoculars or telescope. 'Hinds and calves, wee staggie, hind with a calf and a follower, good stag holding hinds . . .' Is he looking at the same hill? He certainly is. Try again, really concentrate, and eventually you will make out the shapes of deer among the rocks and vegetation. Once you see one, and have a clear idea of shape and scale, you should quickly see others. The mind adjusts to a pattern and can identify similar shapes more easily. Now you are seeing deer, but can you tell what sex they are? What age? And whether a beast is right for culling, or too good, or too young? That's another part of the stalker's job.

It is not enough just to see deer; the stalker has to decide which beasts are shootable. That is to say, which will fit in with his culling policy, and whether there is a realistic possibility of getting to within rifle-range of one of them. You could, of course, set off across the hill to get closer before selecting a victim, but this might mean a lot of extra mileage, especially if the deer you start to stalk turn out to be hinds instead of stags, or perhaps vice versa. Having decided which beast is to be stalked, the stalker will lead the Rifle in the initial approach, using the contours of the ground to get as close as possible before having to crawl or slide along on his belly. Here again, detailed knowledge of the ground may be vital to the success of the stalk.

Even on an apparently bare hillside it is often possible to approach deer to within quite a short distance by putting a ridge or shoulder between them and yourself. As the stalking party gets closer the stalker will have to ensure that they remain unseen, unheard and downwind of the deer. He must judge the range at which his Rifle can be certain of making a clean kill, select a firing position within that distance and get himself and the Rifle to that point undetected. He must make sure the Rifle is comfortable and confident, tell him or her the right moment to shoot and monitor the strike of the bullet to make sure that a killing shot has been made. If by some misfortune a beast should be wounded, the stalker will take the rifle and follow up to make certain that the animal is finished off as quickly and humanely as possible. Sometimes all this may

Winter feeding. Hinds, calves and one young staggie taking hay by the lochside.

be quite straightforward; at others it may be nearly impossible, but the good stalker will endeavour to get a beast for his Rifle whatever the problems.

The complete novice may not appreciate much of what is going on in the course of a stalk. It is quite likely that, at least for his first few times on the hill, he will be so occupied in trying to copy the stalker's progress that he will not have the time to wonder why things are done the way they are. Later, as the novice becomes more familiar with deer, with conditions on the hill and with the problems of stalking, so he should form a greater understanding and appreciation of the skill that is required to lead a successful stalk.

The well-placed shot at the end of the stalk is far from the conclusion of the stalker's duties. Once the beast has been shot it must be gralloched (the stomach and intestines removed), then arrangements have to be made to transport it back to the deer larder. This may mean calling up the ponyman or walking back to collect a vehicle, and if the beast is in an inaccessible place, it may mean dragging it to where it can be loaded on to the pony or in to the vehicle.

When the beast has reached the deer larder, there will be still more work for the stalker to do. The carcase must be weighed then dressed out, ready for the game dealer. This will entail removing the head and feet, separating the pluck (heart, liver and lungs) from the rest of the carcase, cleaning the inside of the carcase and hanging it up to cool. If the meat is required for consumption on the estate, or is to be sent away 'oven-ready' then the stalker will skin and butcher the carcase. The antlers and tusks will be removed and many stalkers supply a jaw bone from every animal to be examined by the experts at the Red Deer Commission who will record the age and size of the stag or hind. If this is to be done then the head must be partly skinned and the jaw removed and boiled to remove all traces of flesh before it is sent to the Commission's offices in Inverness. The Rifle may want the head for a trophy, especially if it is a first stag or a particularly good head, and the task of skinning out and sawing the skull will, of course, fall to the stalker as well.

Feeding on hay. The calf looks quite apprehensive as the young stag squabbles over which bunch of hay to eat.

While out on the hill the stalker is responsible for the safety of his guest and that of anyone else who may be out with the stalking party. He must know what the weather is likely to do, when a mist may clear to allow a stalk to continue or when a cautious retreat from the hill is indicated before conditions worsen. He must also be able to assess the capabilities of his guests and set his own pace to accommodate them; it is no use finding yourself miles from home with darkness falling and one of the party too exhausted to walk a step further.

Clearly then, the stalker has more than enough to occupy his time throughout the stalking season, from mid-summer until the middle of February. What does he do, though, when hind stalking has ended? It is dangerous to generalise, since the work of the stalker both in and out of the season will depend largely on the nature of the forest which he works. Some estates are almost exclusively deer forests – ground which is devoted entirely to red deer stalking with little or no other game. Others may have a stock of grouse and perhaps black game, with a few ptarmigan if the ground is mountainous enough. There may be some low ground stocked with pheasant and partridge, perhaps lochs or esturial waters for wildfowling and woods which will hold woodcock in the autumn and winter. Rabbits and hares can be abundant, particularly the former where there are areas of grassland pasture. There may be sika or roe deer as well as red, and different open seasons apply to these. All or any of these can make demands on the stalker's time, quite apart from the off-season work needed with the red deer stock.

The practice is far from universal, but many estates provide some sort of

107

Heather burning. The easy part of the job is lighting the fire . . .

. . . the hard part is controlling it afterwards. The terrier looks in danger of getting burnt or beaten to death.

winter feed for their deer – hay, sugar-beet nuts, turnips, potatoes or maize – and this must be taken out and distributed daily. In the middle of winter there can be as little as six hours' daylight, so if the feed has to be taken any distance this task alone can occupy a fair proportion of every day. During a particularly severe bout of weather a few years ago, we were taking hay down to feed beasts about three miles from the lodge. There were deep drifts along the road, and we were using a tractor and snow-plough to clear a passage for a van loaded with hay bales. On one memorable occasion we spent an hour clearing three miles of drifts, then a further hour scattering hay and digging out some sheep which were buried under the snow. All the while fresh snow was drifting in on to our tracks to such an extent that it took us a further four hours to plough our way back home. There was little time for anything else that day.

Fine weather in spring will often find the stalker out with broom and matches, burning old heather to encourage the growth of fresh green shoots. This is a particularly necessary job where there are grouse as well as deer, since grouse live almost entirely off heather. Burning for grouse is not just a matter of dropping a match and standing back to admire the flames. Grouse need short heather to feed on, interspersed with longer heather to provide nesting cover and protection from predators. A well burnt moor will have the characteristic patchwork of strips of heather of differing lengths. That pattern will represent many days spent at the hot, smoky job of brooming the edges of the fires.

Heather burning in the Highlands is often a race against time as days when the heather is dry enough to burn and the wind is low enough and in the right direction are all too rare. Crofters and shepherds may have a rather different view of what a proper fire should look like, usually erring on the generous side. Some stalkers wage a constant battle against fires started, officially and unofficially, by others with differing interests on the hill.

There are often fishing as well as shooting interests on a Highland estate. On some rivers, the salmon season opens as early as January and trout fishing starts in mid-March. There may be a full-time or part-time ghillie employed to look after the fishing, but it can equally well be part of the stalker's duties. Much will depend on the quality and quantity of the salmon run. A spate river where fish only run when the river is at a certain level is less likely to have specialist ghillies than one where the fish run throughout the season.

Grouse are not reared in the way that pheasants are, but they still mean plenty of extra work if they are to be encouraged to maintain or increase their numbers. Vermin control is vital to success with grouse and is a year-round task, though perhaps at its busiest in the spring. It is then that fox dens must be checked and the occupants dealt with. A vixen with cubs can account for a lot of grouse when the hens are incubating and rearing chicks. Hooded or carrion crows take a heavy toll of both eggs and chicks during the early summer and weasels, stoats and feral mink will also call for the stalker's attentions at this time of year.

If the grouse are numerous enough to be driven, then maintenance work may be needed on butts. In those places where the birds are shot over pointing dogs, the stalker may have puppies to train or older dogs to get fit ready for the season. The grouse will be left undisturbed during their nesting period from mid-April until early July, but both before and after this time the dogs will probably be busy on the hill. In spring, paired grouse can sit quite well to a pointer and can be invaluable for bringing on a puppy, especially since it is often possible to say, with a fair certainty, where a pair are likely to be found. Once the chicks are strong on the wing, in July, the dogs can be worked, both to get them hardened up ready for the season and to give the stalker an idea of how well his birds have reproduced. A grouse count may be essential where shooting days are let out to tenants in order that a fair number of birds can be 'sold' without over-shooting and damaging the future prospects of the moor.

Pheasants or partridges can be raised in captivity and then released – a more certain way of producing a shootable surplus than relying on nature, but also a more labour-intensive system. If a large number of pheasants are to be raised then it will soon require a full-time keeper to care for them, but many stalkers will rear a few birds, or even a few hundred, to provide a little extra shooting on the low ground at the back end of the season. The chicks have to be fed and protected from predators, then transferred to release pens. The pens themselves must be maintained and feeding and vermin control will become a year-round task. If there is a flight pond for duck it will have to be fed regularly and perhaps the vegetation will need trimming to prevent it clogging up.

Rabbits are sometimes a problem, especially if there are farming activities on the low-ground areas of the forest, so ferreting or shooting them can take up still more time. Often this provides the keeper or stalker with sport and a little extra cash, both welcome during the winter months. A far less pleasant occupation which will affect all keepers and stalkers is the need to guard against the activities of poachers. How much of a stalker's time will be occupied in this unpleasant and sometimes dangerous task will depend primarily on where his

Rabbit control can be an enjoyable part of a stalker's duties when the hind season is over.

forest is situated. The more remote areas may have a comparatively slight incidence of poaching, but an estate which is close to a large urban area may be plagued throughout the year.

Deer poaching can be an exceptionally cruel business as well as, unfortunately, being a very lucrative one. Operating from a car with a spotlight, deer are shot as they graze beside roads at night. A beast can be killed, loaded into a car and be miles away in a matter of minutes – a hopeless task for the stalker who may have sole responsibility for many miles of roads and tracks. Sadly, many of the poaching gangs shoot their victims with shotguns or .22 rifles and many beasts are wounded and left to die lingering and painful deaths. There is no obligation for a poacher to follow up and kill a wounded beast. Indeed, if a beast has been wounded while caught in the beam of a spotlight, it will quickly run out of range of the light, and out of reach of the poacher, even if he were inclined to follow it up.

A .22 rifle will kill an animal the size of a deer, provided that the bullet placement is exact. With such a low powered weapon the margins of error are very small. Consequently many poachers try to kill their victims with a head shot, and any error with the rifle or movement of the animal's head can easily result in a shattered jaw, an injury which will not kill a beast, nor stop it to allow a second shot to be taken. A stag or hind with a broken jaw will quickly be lost in the darkness to die a miserable and cruel death from starvation, perhaps agonising months later.

Poaching is not the romantic and exciting pastime that it is sometimes held up to be; it can be big business for some, and the rewards are such that some poaching gangs are prepared to go to considerable lengths to protect their activities. Assaults on keepers are all too common, sometimes resulting in quite serious injury, though changes in the law in Scotland in 1982 have meant that the courts can take a more serious view of deer poaching. It is probably the least welcome part of a stalker's profession, but one that is likely to remain as long as there are deer on the hill.

There may be other stock to be tended in addition to the deer. If the estate still uses ponies these will have to be cared for throughout the year, as will the stalker's dogs – pointers, terriers, collies and perhaps spaniels and retrievers if there is low-ground shooting. There may be sheep on the hill as well as deer, and stalkers are often involved to a greater or lesser extent in their welfare. He may act as shepherd himself, or be asked to assist with lambing, clipping and dipping.

Recent years have seen a greater and greater amount of scientific and semi-scientific research being undertaken in the Highlands. The Game Conservancy are running a grouse research project, looking for the reasons why grouse stocks have declined in some areas. The work takes several forms including the radio tracking of individual birds fitted with miniature transmitters, and the collecting of blood samples from shot birds in order to test for louping-ill antibodies. The stalker will, of course, be involved in both these projects and may also be assisting the Red Deer Commission in their work. The Commission organises deer counts in late winter, usually soon after hind stalking has ended, in order that it may monitor changes in the overall deer population of Scotland. A

Tagging calves in June. The stalker circles warily around a new born calf, landing net at the ready.

Still confident in its camouflage, the calf does not move, even as the net is about to go over it.

A deer calf is a beautiful animal – velvety nose, huge ears and big, dark eyes.

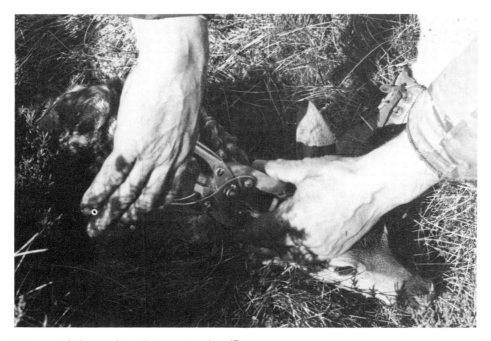

Using special pliers to clip a plastic tag into the calf's ear.

Tag in place, the stalker gently settles the calf down in the heather to wait for the hind returning.

Another tagged calf, quite calm despite having been handled and having a tag clipped into its ear.

count will involve both the officers of the Commission and the stalkers from the area being counted, working in concert to cover the ground as thoroughly as possible.

The Nature Conservancy Council, the Royal Society for the Protection of Birds and many other bodies have interests in the birds, animals and plants of the Highlands, and may work with (or at times, against) the keepers and stalkers in pursuing their interests. Often there is mutual respect and co-operation between stalkers and scientists, but this is not always the case.

It is in the nature of their job that many stalkers will be excellent naturalists. That a man chooses to become a professional stalker in the first place shows that he must have at least an interest in natural history. Stalking involves many hours spent out on the hills, not just wandering around with eyes on the ground, but watching, and really observing what is going on. The main objective will be to see what the deer are doing, but it is impossible to miss seeing a great deal of other wildlife, not, in any case, that one would choose to miss it. A man who has spent his whole life out on the hill may well be wary of a biology or zoology graduate who comes straight from a city university and tries to tell him how to do his job. Equally, there are those who resent any contact with bodies such as the NCC or RSPB, seeing it as unwarranted interference in their work.

There is no clear right or wrong in many cases, but it seems certain that the future will mean an even greater involvement, by the NCC in particular, and the creation of more and more SSSIs (Sites of Special Scientific Interest) throughout the Highlands. Since the process is probably inevitable, it may be as well for all stalkers and proprietors to ensure that they work with, rather than against, officialdom, trying to influence matters for the good from within rather than fighting from the outside – a battle that is almost certain to fail.

Living in comparative isolation, as many stalkers do, tends to force man to become very self-reliant. Services to the more remote regions of Scotland can be very poor and often, if something breaks it is up to the stalker to fix it. Many estates rely on their own generating plants to supply electricity and this will have to be serviced, as will any estate vehicles and machinery. Some can take self-sufficiency to quite extraordinary lengths. One stalker, on a large estate in the east of Scotland, actually built his own hydro-electric generator and wired up his house for lighting and power. I understand that the same man built his own rifle, using a half-shaft from a Land Rover as the basis for the barrel. It is probably unnecessary to add that he loads his own cartridges for use in the rifle. Obviously he is exceptional, but many a stalker will happily tackle a problem that would find most men telephoning for expert advice and assistance; and as often as not they will find a solution.

Whatever other calls may be made upon his time, be it different branches of shooting sport, fishing, farming or general repairs, the primary concern of every stalker is the well-being of 'his' deer. He may be out alone, night after night, keeping watch for poachers or sitting by a fox den waiting for a vixen to come within rifle-range. A winter's day might find him battling snow-drifts and freezing winds to scatter hay and turnips for his stags to eat. Some stalkers will monitor the birth weights and sexes of new-born calves, perhaps ear tagging

115

them as well so that they may be identified as they mature. There is a great deal of behind the scenes work that goes on, unsuspected by the guest who goes to the hill for a stag. Some of it may have a direct bearing on the success or failure of the stalk, some will be concerned with other matters entirely.

There is no point in trying to generalise the role, or the nature, of stalkers. It is true to say, however, that, particularly where the novice is concerned, a good stalker can do a tremendous amount to increase the enjoyment of first days on the hill. It is all too easy to stalk deer by tagging along in the professional stalker's wake, walking when he walks, crawling where he crawls and moving up at the last moment to take the rifle and shoot whichever beast is indicated. You will have been deer stalking, that is true, but there is little satisfaction if all you have seen all day is the back of a stalker's neck, or the soles of his boots. How much better to become involved in the day, to listen to and perhaps even question the plan of campaign. If you can appreciate why things are done as well as how they are done, then you are well on your way to attaining some sort of proficiency as an amateur stalker, and you will enjoy your sport far more as a result.

Although I suggested questioning the stalker, it is important to choose the right time and place. The time to seek enlightenment on the correct culling ratio of hinds to stags is not when you are lying in full view of a big, switch-topped stag whose suspicions are already aroused and who is about to depart the scene at high speed. It is also important to listen, and listen carefully, so that you don't act until you are sure what is required of you – especially if your actions involve firing the rifle.

Just before the rut a few years ago, a stalker and his Rifle had crawled to within range of a sizable bunch of stags. They were a mixed lot – several young staggies, a ten pointer who was going back, a switch-topped six pointer and a royal. The stalker decided that the ten pointer should be taken and instructed the Rifle accordingly, adding that there might be a chance at a second beast if the shot didn't put the rest to immediate flight. John H., the Rifle, took his time, shot straight, and killed the ten pointer. The rest of the stags stood up, looking round uncertainly but not yet ready for precipitate flight. The switch-topped stag was standing next to the royal. The stalker whispered his instructions. 'Take the one on the left of the royal.' At least, that is what he had intended to say. He had only got as far as ' . . . the one on the left . . .' when a second shot rang out and the stag which had been standing on the left of the fallen ten pointer joined his erstwhile companion on the heather. Needless to say, it was the royal, not the switch. History does not record what was said in the next few moments. In any event, there was nothing that could be done once the trigger had been squeezed. The royal's head (he was actually a thirteen pointer) is hanging in the gunroom to this day, adorned by another of those little poems which appear from time to time.

> Behold, my friend, John's trophy head,
> Which, not intended to be dead,
> Must blame its current situation,
> On problems in communication.

8

The Stalk

Stalking is not a skill that can be learnt from a book. To become a competent stalker on the open hill requires practice, not theory, though an understanding of what you are trying to do will obviously be of benefit. Fortunately for those who would like to try their hand at Highland deer stalking the system in operation on practically all deer forests allows even the complete beginner to go to the hill with every chance of success.

In order to be able to approach to within rifle-range of deer consistently undetected, the stalker must have both a good general knowledge of the way that deer behave, and a more specific understanding of the conditions on his particular forest. Deer everywhere behave in a broadly similar manner when they sense a threat. Their eyes, ears and especially their noses are early warning systems, constantly looking, listening and scenting the breeze for any hint of danger. When they feel threatened, their defence is simply to put some distance between themselves and the threat.

The manner in which they take their leave will depend on how immediate they believe the danger to be. Sometimes they may gently amble across the hill, stopping to pull a mouthful of feed as they go and showing no real signs of alarm. On another occasion their reaction may be one of headlong flight – a plunging gallop that may carry them a hundred yards or a half mile before they slow again. This difference in response may depend on which of their senses alerts them to danger. There are no hard and fast rules where deer are concerned; when they can see humans at a distance they will be content to watch, keeping a wary eye on the figures but not actually moving off unless they consider that the threat has increased. This may be because the humans have come too close for comfort, or it may be because the deer have lost sight of them behind a hill or in a burn bottom. As long as the threat is clearly visible the deer may be content to keep a watching brief. If they lose sight of the thing that is threatening them they are far more likely to retreat, even though the danger has not yet intruded into their flight space.

In much the same way, deer will very quickly be off if they wind man but cannot see him, or if they hear a strange and unidentified sound. Again, there are no rules; the merest whisper of the rifle cover against a rock may clear every beast from a face; a rifle shot which kills one beast out of bunch may do no more than bring the rest of the deer to their feet. Long experience of deer will endow the observant stalker with a sixth sense which tells him when he can take a risk in moving closer, or when one more liberty will cause precipitate flight.

Perhaps even more important than knowledge of the ways of deer is

of them, provided they have seen me coming. If a stag happens to be grazing with his back to me, and I approach upwind, so that he is not alerted by my scent, then he is likely to make a headlong dash for safety when he suddenly catches sight of me. If he is one of the regular feeders, the dash will probably cover no more than

practice will enable the professional stalker to assess beasts very quickly and
accurately. A good stalker can tell at a glance the age and bodily condition of

a few yards before dignity is restored, but in those few moments his alarm will
have been passed on to every other beast in the vicinity. Even those which had
quite calmly watched me pass will start to run as soon as the startled one does.
Fear is quickly transmitted from one beast to another.

The problem for the stalker then, once he begins to make his approach to the
deer, is to get close without being seen, heard or winded by his intended victim,
or by any other deer which are in the area. It is not enough simply to stalk the
beast you are planning to shoot, you must, in effect, stalk every beast in the
corrie or on the face.

The eyes and ears of the red deer are at least as good and possibly better than
those of the humans who stalk them. If you can see or hear the deer, then it is a
safe bet that they will be able to see or hear you. Scenting is rather different. The
human nose is as a club to a scalpel in comparison to the scenting powers of deer.
The stalker and I were lying out near the march one day watching a bunch of
hinds in a little valley below us. They were clearly agitated; all their heads were
up, and they kept looking nervously back across the march, which was directly
upwind from them. They gradually moved away, eventually crossing in front of
us and dropping down the face towards the loch. There was nothing among them
worth shooting so we just lay and watched them until they were out of sight.
Some time after the last hind had vanished we saw a stalking party from the
neighbouring estate, fully half a mile and perhaps nearer three quarters of a mile
away over the march. Even at that range, the deer had winded them, and been
sufficiently alarmed to drift away from the threat of danger. Indeed, it is possible
that deer rely more on their sense of smell than on either sight or hearing to warn
them of the approach of danger.

When beginning the approach, it is necessary to bear three things in mind.

*The shot. The stalker checks the result through his telescope while the Rifle stays in the
prone position in case a second shot might be needed. (It wasn't.)*

Will I be within sight of the deer? Will I be making any sound that they might hear? And, perhaps most importantly, is the breeze, at any time, going to blow from me towards the deer? Sound must be regulated by the stalkers themselves. Wearing the right clothes will help as will taking great care not to kick a loose stone, rattle your stick against a rock or splash your boots in a pool.

It is sometimes impossible to stay out of sight altogether, but this does not mean that the stalk is necessarily doomed to failure. It is movement that attracts the eye, and by staying absolutely still whenever a beast is looking towards you and moving only when all the heads are turned away or bent to feed, it may still be possible to approach to within range. Indeed, such an approach, within full view of the deer, can be among the most exciting and satisfying of stalking. However, if the breeze should carry your scent across to the deer, then the stalk is probably going to fail. If deer are warned by their noses that there are humans about, and worse, unseen humans, then they will almost certainly move away – perhaps a gentle drift off along the hill, perhaps a loping trot that will carry them right off the beat and possibly right off the forest. The very first thing to consider then, when planning your stalk, is the direction of the wind.

Wind direction is not just a simple matter of wetting your finger and holding it up to test the breeze. Although the wind may seem to be blowing quite steadily from a particular quarter, the geography of the ground can play some peculiar tricks with wind direction. Where the wind blows over the crest of a ridge, it can eddy through one hundred and eighty degrees. It may be blowing down the

The end result. The Rifle with a good cull beast, just losing the velvet from his antlers.

127

slope at the top of the hill, and at the bottom, but turning to blow back uphill half-way down the face. Where the wind is swirling around a corrie it may blow in half a dozen different directions at once, making an absolute nonsense of any attempt to get to within rifle-range of a beast. It is here that the local knowledge and long experience of the stalker will be invaluable. If you are a stranger to the ground and attempt a stalk under these conditions, then the first warning that you may get that all is not well is usually the feel of the wind on the back of your neck. Almost at once the deer will have their heads up, testing the breeze and looking around nervously for the source of the threatening scent. An old hind may bark a warning, then your quarry will be off, and you will have to think again.

The experienced stalker, however, will probably have a good idea of the tricks that the wind is likely to play, and may have a trick or two of his own to defeat it. In the same way, when you look at beasts grazing on a bare and featureless face, it may seem that it would be impossible to approach them without being in full view. Even so, the contour of the ground may provide cover once you are on the same level, or perhaps a higher level, than the deer. The first approach may actually have to be made by turning your back and going away from your intended victim.

It is sometimes the case that you, or the deer, will have a clearer view of the ground below than the ground above. If this is the case, then it is obviously better for you to have the benefit of the high ground and to leave the deer with the restricted view. So, once you have finished your spy and selected a beast to stalk, your first move may be to retreat to a point out of sight of the deer, then climb the hill until you are above their level. Once you have sufficient height you can come back along above the deer, getting much closer but remaining safely out of view.

As you approach at your new level, it is vital that you should see the deer, or fix the place where they are (hopefully) still grazing, before they see you. The whole look of the hill may change as you climb up – your horizon rises with you and the relation of one point to another will also alter. The rock which looked so prominent from below may be just one more boulder among a hundred when you have climbed up to it. You need a good mark that can be positively identified at your new level, and you need to proceed with the greatest caution as you near it. Once you have actually located the deer again the problem becomes a little more clear-cut.

The initial approach has something of the flavour of grand strategy. You may put the whole of a mountainside between yourself and the deer and then march happily along, quite secure from detection, provided there aren't a few beasts you overlooked when spying, whose paths you are about to cross. Once you get to within contact distance of your target then the strategy must give way to some tactical manoeuvring.

This is the part that you may have read about in descriptions of deer stalking. Crawling up a burn with water running in at your neck and out by your boots. Lying face down in a peat hag while a wary old hind gazes suspiciously towards you. Slithering on your belly to gain the dubious cover of a tiny tussock of

Who was most surprised, stag or stalkers? There may be beasts lying unseen in dead ground between you and the object of your stalk.

heather. Frozen motionless in full sight of every beast on the face, waiting interminably for them to settle down and resume their grazing. Seeing the stag you intend to shoot driven away from his hinds by a rival with far too good a head to be culled. Having a horde of midges feasting on your neck and not being able to shoo them away without being seen and ruining the stalk. Lying for an hour in the snow while you wait for that big switch to stand up and give you a decent shot at him. It can be any of those, or any one of a thousand things; all different, all exciting, some exhilarating and some just plain cold and uncomfortable.

The first rule is to do exactly what the stalker tells you. The odds are that you will be following him and doing just the same as he does. If that's what you are told, then that is exactly what is required of you. If the stalker is hip-deep in a bog hole you may be sure he is there because it is necessary. If he moves bent over double, then you must move bent over double. If he crawls on his hands and knees, then you must crawl on your hands and knees. If he elects to lie face down in a wet peat hag then you had better be face down in the dirt as well when you reach it. And, most vital of all, if he suddenly freezes into complete immobility you must do the same – immediately. The odds are that a stag or hind is looking straight at you.

What will happen on this final approach must depend on conditions on the day – the wind, the position of the deer, how close you must get in order to have a clear shot, whether the beasts are settled or whether they are about to take off at any moment. In a light breeze the slightest sound can carry far enough to warn the deer; on a good gusty day you may be able to get away with quite a lot of noise. Mist and drizzle obscure the deer's vision as well as obscuring yours, and may either help or hinder depending on circumstances.

If you are out with a good, experienced stalker, then he will make the decisions for you, particularly if you are a beginner to stalking. Listen carefully, do your best to do exactly as the expert tells you, and make sure that you emulate him as you creep and crawl into range. He may be making the plans and putting them into operation, but the deer will be just as quick to run away if they catch a glimpse of you. You will be told what to do, but you still have to do it, and do it properly, if the stalk is to be a success. Assuming that all goes according to plan, and there is no guarantee that it will, even with the best stalker in the world, then sooner or later you will reach the chosen firing point, the rifle will be eased into your hands, and then it is up to you. When the stalker says, 'Take him now', the success or failure of the day is firmly in your hands. In the next chapter we will look at ways to try and ensure that you will be successful.

9
The Shot

If all has gone according to plan with the stalk, then sooner or later the moment arrives when you are within rifle-range of your intended victim, the stalker passes you the rifle and you are ready to take the shot. It is the natural culmination of all that has gone before, and for the first time even the most inexperienced stalker is on his or her own. The professional stalker has done his job, and now he will be watching to see that you do your part correctly. Considered logically, it is not a difficult task. The target area on a stag allows a considerable margin of error, and provided the Rifle is neither careless through over-confidence, nor affected by stag fever, then there is no reason to miss.

Having said that, everyone does miss, sooner or later, no matter how good a rifle shot they may be. The beast may make a sudden move just as you are about to squeeze the trigger or you may have been inadvertently resting the barrel against a stone and caused the rifle to shoot high. The sights could have taken a knock, there may even be a fault in the ammunition. Even more likely, the shot may have been hurried, the shooter may have flinched or, most likely of all, become a little careless through over-confidence. It can happen to everyone. If it happens to you, then try and assess what it was you did wrong, make sure that you don't do it again, then forget it. Confidence is vital to good shooting and you should always concentrate on the shot you are about to take. Never allow yourself to fret over the one you have just missed.

Perhaps the first thing to consider, before even thinking about the actual shot, is what you are trying to do and how you can best do it. The aim of the stalker is to kill his beast *as quickly and cleanly as possible*. We have already looked at the reasons why an annual cull of the red deer is necessary. If a proportion of the deer population is not culled every year, then there would quickly be heavy annual losses through starvation. A properly planned and executed cull will minimise these losses and take a valuable protein crop at the same time. It is in the best interests of the deer themselves that a cull should be taken every year, but there is no excuse for causing unnecessary suffering in so doing. Which brings us back to the deer stalker's motto – 'as quickly and cleanly as possible'.

Let us begin by considering how best we can kill an animal the size of a red deer. Since the deer are wild animals, the use of a humane killer, which has to be fired when in contact with the animal's head, is out of the question. A rifle is the next best thing, and will allow a competent shot to kill a beast with near certainty at distances of up to two hundred yards and even a bit over, provided that bullet placement is accurate.

A bullet can kill an animal for several different reasons. If severe damage is done to a major nerve centre such as the brain, or upper spinal chord, then death will follow almost immediately, as the functions of the respiratory and circulatory systems are terminated. Damage to the heart or a major blood vessel will cause rapid death from bleeding and loss of blood to the brain. Damage to minor blood vessels may also cause death from bleeding, though it will be some time before death occurs, and a wound which bursts the stomach will cause slow death from blood poisoning as the stomach contents are spilled into the body cavity. Other wounds – broken legs and broken jaws included – will cause a great deal of needless suffering from which the unfortunate animal may possibly recover.

It follows that we must endeavour to hit either a major nerve centre or a major blood vessel with our bullet. All the points on a deer which will guarantee rapid death if struck by a bullet with sufficient energy are in the front third of the animal. A shot which strikes the brain will kill a beast instantly, as will one which severs the spinal column in the neck. A shot through the chest cavity will cause almost certain death through damage to lungs, heart or major arteries. Any shot which strikes further back than the diaphragm *may* cause the eventual death of the animal, but not quickly enough to meet our criterion of a clean and rapid kill.

A head shot might seem the obvious choice; but it is not. The brain of a deer is quite small in relation to the size of the head, and far from an easy target. A stag or hind can move its head slightly at any time, without any warning. A tiny movement from the beast, or a slight error in aiming, and the result will be an animal with a smashed jaw or a shattered nose – an animal, moreover, which will be quite capable of getting up and running off at a far faster pace than the stalker can hope to follow. If you do not manage to catch up and administer a killing shot, and there is every possibility that you will not, then that animal is condemned to a long and painful existence before death puts a merciful end to its suffering.

Stalking during the rut is very exciting. A very dark stag, roaring during late October.

Broadside-on, and ideally placed for a chest shot. The vital areas for the stalker are all in the front third of a beast.

The shot will almost certainly be taken from the prone position, with the left hand resting firmly on the ground for maximum steadiness.

Head shots should never be attempted, with two possible exceptions. If a beast has been wounded, and is lying in such a position that only a head shot is possible, then such a shot may be justified. If a beast is lying with its back to you, then a shot at the axis bone, where the neck joins the skull, is permissible. If you shoot high you will either hit the brain or miss altogether; if low, the bullet will break the neck, and if you are off to either side you will miss cleanly. Otherwise head shots are out, no matter how clever you may be with a rifle. Try them, and sooner or later you will shoot away the face from a beast without killing it, and no animal should suffer such a fate.

The neck shot is a rather different matter. A bullet which strikes the spinal column anywhere along the length of the neck will cause almost instant death, either by severing the spinal chord, or by causing such severe shock to the nerves in the chord that both breathing and circulation will cease. A neck shot usually results in either instant death or a clean miss, though it is possible to hit the fleshy portion of the neck without damaging any of the vital areas, particularly with a stag whose neck is swollen during the rut. The neck shot is much favoured by stalkers who are shooting for the kitchen or the deep-freeze since it damages a minimum of meat and makes skinning an easier task than does a chest shot. However, the neck is undeniably a smaller, and therefore a more difficult, target than the chest area, and there is always the danger of a beast moving its neck just as the shot is taken. For these reasons the most usual shot, particularly for the novice stalker, is the chest shot, normally taken broadside-on.

The chest cavity contains the heart, lungs and major blood vessels. A soft-pointed bullet entering the chest will cause a great deal of damage as it expands, or fragments, and very rapid bleeding will result. A shot in the centre of the chest will cause damage to the front of the lungs, and perhaps the aorta. The heart, which lies low down in the chest cavity, will continue to pump blood, assuming that it is not itself hit, and this pumping action will actually speed the animal's death as it draws blood away from the brain and other vital organs pumping it out through the wounds in the lungs. Bleeding is further exacerbated by the action of the diaphragm which, in attempting to draw air into the lungs, will actually draw blood out from the wound. If the heart itself is struck then bleeding will be slower and death, though certain, will take a little longer since the pumping action of the heart is lost.

A high shot which breaks the spine will knock the animal down instantly and cause rapid death, provided the spinal column is severed. The danger with a chest shot is a low bullet strike which breaks a front leg, or a shot placed too far back which strikes the animal in the stomach – a gut shot which will definitely not cause a quick and clean death. However, the target area for the chest shot is of considerable size – perhaps a foot wide by fifteen inches high – so, provided that you aim correctly, a shot which strikes within six inches of your aiming point, in any direction, should give the desired result. It is most important to emphasise, however, that the fact that there is a fair amount of leeway *does not* mean that the Rifle can be casual about the shot. Always aim to be as precise as possible. Careless shooting accounts for nearly all missed or wounded beasts.

The actual shot will almost invariably be taken from the prone position, lying face downwards being the steadiest way of firing a rifle, short of clamping it in a vice. Target shots take their weight on their elbows, with their hands clear of the ground, but the stalking rifleman is not bound by target rules and should ensure that his left hand (for a right-handed shot) is resting firmly on whatever may be available. You will often be lying behind a heathery knoll or a tussock of grass, and if so you can plant your hand firmly down on this to ensure that you have the steadiest platform possible to shoot from. If you need a little more elevation for your left hand, then a telescope case or the rolled-up rifle cover may be sufficient to raise the hand enough to bring the sights to bear. Get as comfortable as possible with the rifle firmly into your shoulder, feet spread apart and left hand firmly supported. When you look through the sights, the picture should be as steady and still as you can possibly make it. Make sure that there are no tufts of heather or grass in front of the rifle muzzle but below the line of sight. It only takes a very small object to deflect a high-velocity bullet, and even a heather sprig may be enough to cause it to break up in flight.

When you are firmly and comfortably settled, sure that there are no unwanted bits of vegetation in front of the muzzle, and getting a good, clear view of your stag or hind through the sights, then ease the safety catch off, take a couple of deep breaths to calm yourself and, very gently, squeeze the trigger. If you have done everything correctly then your beast is as good as dead.

Rifle shooting should be a calm and steady business. Never hurry unless you are trying to stop a wounded beast which is about to vanish from sight. If you rush, then you will tend to snatch at the trigger and the bullet will not go where you intended. However, once you are comfortable and steady and your sights are properly settled on target, then there is nothing to be gained by waiting. The longer you try to hold your aim the less steady you will become. Never confuse 'not rushing' with waiting just for the sake of waiting. If your left hand is firmly anchored, you have a steady grip of the fore end and butt, you are comfortable in your firing position and the sight picture looks right, then there is no reason to wait. If everything is right, then shoot him.

The sight picture is all-important. As we have seen, if you are taking a broadside-on chest shot, you have a target about a foot square. A bullet placed anywhere in that square foot is a killing shot. That is your margin of error, but it is vital that you concentrate on *exact* placement of your bullet, not on putting it somewhere around the target area. It is all too easy to sight on the stag as a whole instead of concentrating on the one tiny area where you intend the bullet to strike.

First-class shotgun users often talk about hitting their quarry in the head. If the charge from a twelve-bore shotgun has spread to cover something in excess of a thirty-inch diameter circle at forty yards range, then a shot which centres that charge exactly on a pheasant's head will also put a fair number of pellets into the body. A novice shoots at the pheasant, not at any particular part of it, and is less successful as a result. The expert does not actually shoot his birds in the head, but because he concentrates on the head he forces himself to shoot more exactly and therefore more accurately. By the same token, if you aim at an area twelve inches square on the side of a stag and miss by three or four inches to one side or the other, then you will either miss altogether, or hit the beast in the gut. If however, you concentrate on a very precise bullet placement, in the exact centre of your target area, then an error of three or four inches in any direction will still ensure a clean kill.

Opinions differ as to where the best aiming point is for a chest shot (sometimes called a heart shot or a body shot). A low aiming point will hit the heart, if accurate, a shot at the top of the withers will break the spine at the base of the neck and a shot through the shoulders will take the forward part of the lungs, but

The aim of every stalker. A good, cull beast, quickly and cleanly killed by a single, well placed shot.

spoil a lot of meat into the bargain. My own preference is for a shot right into the centre of the killing area, thus giving the maximum margin of error in all directions. Follow up the back edge of the foreleg, keep going until you are midway between brisket and spine, and put your bullet there.

If you are accurate, the deer will probably jerk to the shot, run for a few yards, then fall as the blood supply to its brain fails. If you shoot a little low and strike the heart then the time from shot to death will be considerably longer, and the animal may well cover a fair bit of ground before going down. I believe this is because the pumping action of the heart has been stopped abruptly by the bullet and the blood in the brain and lungs can remain there for rather longer than if the heart were still beating. In either case the result will be the same and death will follow quickly and certainly.

A shot which strikes a little forward may break one or both shoulders, resulting in a swift collapse, the beast kicking on the ground for a few seconds before dying. If your bullet is high and strikes the spine then the animal will collapse immediately. Beware of a beast that does this; it is possible that the bullet may have caused temporary paralysis to the nerves in the spinal column, but not actually severed the spinal chord. If this is the case there is a chance that the animal may get to its feet again and require a second shot to prevent it from escaping. Whenever a beast collapses immediately to a chest shot, reload the rifle and be prepared to take another shot if the stalker orders you.

A deer which is unfortunate enough to be hit too far back, gut shot, will run off, but probably stop and either lie down, or stand looking very hunched and miserable. If it has gone too far to allow a second shot to be taken it may be best to allow it to settle, and stalk it for a second time. If you allow it to see you it may move off for a considerable distance. Finally, if your shot is low and breaks a leg this should be immediately obvious, and every effort must be made to finish off the unfortunate animal as quickly as possible. A stag or hind is capable of covering a long distance, and at a far greater pace than a man, even on three legs. As a rough rule of thumb, if a front leg is broken the beast is more likely to go uphill; if a back leg is damaged then downhill progress is easier.

The stalker will be watching through his telescope to see where the bullet strikes and will also be guided by the sound, and the actions of the animal in telling whether the shot will quickly prove fatal, or whether further action is required. If the latter should be the case, then he will either ask you to take a second shot or, perhaps more likely, take the rifle himself and finish the job. However, assuming that you have got it right, and most people do if they take their time and stay calm, then by now you should have a dead stag or hind lying on the heather.

The first thing to do after taking the shot, successful or not, is to reload the rifle. You are then ready for a second shot if the beast should only be wounded, or if the stalker decides that there is another animal within range which should be culled. This happened the very first time I shot a stag. We had had a long, uphill stalk after a stag which was holding hinds above us. The problem was with the hinds rather than the stag, who was too preoccupied with affairs of the heart to take any notice of us, but eventually we got to our firing point, he obliged by

Gralloching. Begin by bleeding the beast. Stick it with your knife just above the breast bone . . .

standing broadside on, and I shot him through the chest. He ran off strongly at the shot, then staggered and collapsed about sixty yards away from where I had shot him. As he was going down, a second stag appeared over the ridge of the hill and prepared to attack 'my' beast. Before the newcomer could make his presence felt the original stag had died, so the second stag came on down the hill to take over the hinds. His hopes were soon dashed though. Ronald the stalker decided that this beast also qualified as a shootable stag, so I ended my first day at stags with a right and left.

The more usual reason for not leaping to your feet and tossing your hat in the air at a successful shot is that it is better to allow any other deer in the vicinity to move away quietly, if they are so minded, rather than disturbing them unnecessarily. Eventually, when any other beasts are out of sight and he is quite certain that the shot beast is dead, the stalker will take back the rifle, unload if necessary, then slip it back into its cover. You may now have a closer look at 'your' stag.

The first thing to do when reaching a dead stag or hind is to make quite certain that it is actually dead. This can be done by touching the end of your stick against the eyeball. If there is no reaction then the animal is dead. The next thing to do is to bleed and gralloch it.

The gralloch is usually the responsibility of the stalker, but it is quite a simple and straightforward operation, and anyone who stalks should know how to do it, and be prepared to do it if necessary. Provided the animal has not been shot in the stomach it is not a particularly messy, or bloody task. Different stalkers have

. . . then use your foot to pump the diaphragm and aid the bleeding process. Not all stalkers bleed a beast this way.

their own methods of gralloching a beast, but the end result should be the same whatever procedure is followed. Some bleed before they gralloch, some after and some not at all. The choice is yours.

You can bleed a deer by sticking it with your knife, just above the top of the breast bone. Keep the knife in the wound and use your boot to pump the chest, which will help the flow of blood out of the chest cavity. Alternatively, wait until you have removed the stomach and intestines, then slit the diaphragm and release the blood through the stomach cavity, or leave it inside until you get back to the larder. With a chest shot beast it will have already been effectively bled from the effects of the wound; all you are doing is releasing the blood from the chest cavity. If you have killed your beast with a neck shot though, bleeding is more important since there will have been comparatively little blood loss from the bullet wound.

Before gralloching, the correct procedure is to tie off the oesophagus so that the stomach contents will not spill out as it is removed. Make a slit along the length of the throat and locate the gullet. Scrape the flesh away from an inch or two of the gullet, then cut it off and tie a knot in it. The scraped portion will allow the knot to hold without slipping. In practice many stalkers do not do this, but it is the correct procedure and should prevent any accidental spillage of the stomach contents into the body cavity – something which can very rapidly sour the meat.

To gralloch, begin by turning the animal on to its back, then make a slit down the length of the stomach from sternum to groin. Take care when cutting that you do not receive a blow in your face from an involuntary kick of a hind leg. This sort of nervous movement can occur for quite some time after death, and a sharp hoof may inflict quite a nasty wound. The other problem which can occur with this initial cut is the knife going too deep and opening the stomach. If you pinch up a fold of skin near the sternum to make your original cut, then put the fingers of your free hand inside the body cavity on either side of the knife point, then you should be able to slit open the belly without cutting into the stomach itself.

Once you have made your cut, lay the animal on its right side, at which point part of the stomach will probably flop out through the hole. Reach in over the top of the stomach and grasp the spleen, pull it out and discard it. Then feel for the narrowing at the opening of the stomach where the oesophagus enters, and pull this away from the diaphragm, bringing the rest of the gullet with it. The whole stomach can then be removed from the beast along with much of the intestines. Follow the line of the bowel back towards the vent, and pull it away as near to the vent as possible, taking care not to spill any of the contents inside the carcase. If you have not already bled the beast by sticking it in the chest, then now is the moment to bleed the chest cavity through the rear of the diaphragm. If you are saving the gralloch for dog food, slit it open and shake out the contents, then rinse it out if there is a pool or burn nearby. That done, the stag or hind is ready for transport back to the deer larder. The Red Deer Commission publish an excellent wall chart which gives details of the correct method of gralloching and cleaning a carcase, complete with easy-to-follow diagrams.

Once the gralloch has been completed it is time to call up the ponyman, or to return and collect the transport and load up the carcase. There may be time to go after another stag or hind, or the shot may have signalled the end of business for the day. Obviously, much will depend on the amount of time the first stalk has taken, the culling policy of the particular forest you are stalking on, and how late in the day it may be. It is never advisable to start a stalk as darkness is falling. If the shot should be off target and a wounded animal result there may be no time to follow it up and kill it before darkness falls, and a hurried shot taken in fading light is a sure recipe for disaster.

The business of deciding which beasts are to be shot is a vital part of the stalker's responsibilities, and it is an extremely skilled task. There is a natural mortality among any animal population, including man and everything has to die eventually. The aim of the stalker is to shoot those animals which would have died anyway and then to further reduce the population so that the remaining beasts have sufficient winter feed to sustain them through to spring. One test for a cull beast is to look for those which are out of condition either through old age or illness, or for calves (during hind stalking) that are small or weak and therefore unlikely to survive the winter. There is no point in shooting a healthy beast while leaving a sickly one to die a natural death from starvation.

It is common policy among estate owners (though not an invariable one) to try and improve the overall deer stock by culling out the smaller beasts and stags with poor heads, leaving the biggest and best antlered stags to breed with the biggest and best hinds. This is in direct contrast to the Victorian system of killing off the best animals in order to secure trophy heads to hang on the walls of their shooting lodges. There are still some forests which cull the best out as a matter of course, particularly where the stalking is leased to continental sportsmen who are willing to pay heavily for a trophy head.

In general though, the policy is to cull out those stags which have poor heads. Into this category fall hummels (beasts with no antlers at all) and switches (beasts with a single long point on either side, or a single point above the brow points). The problem for the stalker is to decide whether a beast is a mature stag with a poor head, and thus a desirable cull, or a young beast whose head will improve if left – a simple task if the two are seen together and body size can be compared, but much less easy if the beast in question is on its own. A stag which is getting old may still have a very respectable set of antlers, but be considered suitable for culling since he may not over-winter successfully, or be capable of holding hinds the next year if he does survive.

The selection of hinds for culling is even more difficult, since they have no antlers to guide the stalker in his choice. Here he will be considering coat and condition as well as age, and will look at how well her calf, if any, is doing. An old hind who can rear a calf through winter is worth leaving; if the calf is too weak or sickly, then both are better out of the way.

On a well managed forest, it may be necessary to kill a number of quite healthy beasts in order to hold overall numbers at a level compatible with winter grazing. There are several theoretical systems of culling, based on ideal sex ratios, and number of trophy animals to be left to maturity. While such systems may look very attractive on paper, and indeed will probably work out more or less as planned with beasts in the confines of a deer park, they may be impossible to operate on the open hill. The deer on the majority of forests have freedom of movement over the marches and, particularly during the rut, stags may wander for many miles. If you are stalking a hind forest, then the only stags which will be shot are those which arrive on the ground in pursuit of hinds during the rut. Obviously, there can be no pre-planned culling selection when the stalker has no control over which stags, or how many, will be on his ground during the stalking season.

Likewise, a stag which spends most of the year on your ground may disappear over the march when the rut begins. You then have no control over whether he will be culled by one of your neighbours. How can this be allowed for in a pre-planned culling policy? Much must depend on the particular forest, the amount of movement across the marches, and the relationship of the owner, and the stalker, with their neighbours. 'He's not one of ours, we may as well shoot him,' is not an uncommon sentiment among stalkers.

While it is very simple to draw up charts showing how many beasts from each age group should be shot, it is very different, when confronted with a bunch of perhaps fifty hinds and calves, to quickly and accurately assess which should be culled and which should be left for another year. It can be almost as hard to try to explain to a guest exactly which one of the fifty animals milling about in front of him is the one he should shoot. At least a stag has a simple distinguishing feature fixed to the top of his head. To a good and experienced professional stalker a

Slit open the belly, using your spare hand to guide the knife and ensure that the stomach itself is not pierced.

Pulling out the stomach through the gralloching cut.

With the stomach removed the rest of the intestines can be pulled out.

Some stalkers prefer to bleed their beasts through the back of the diaphragm, after the gralloch is complete.

bunch of beasts will be as easy to read as a book. He will know their age and condition, which calf belongs to which hind and which beasts are likely to succumb in a hard winter. He will be able to tell this quickly, easily, and probably without knowing precisely *how* he knows. It requires long years of practice and is not a skill that can be easily acquired. The best the novice stalker can do is to look hard, listen carefully, and do his utmost to ensure that the beast he shoots really is the one the stalker intended.

When the carcase is loaded on to the pony or into the Argo then the party can make their way back to the deer larder. Once home is reached the guest is free to find himself a hot bath and a glass of something warming, but there is still work for the stalker to do. I shall look at larder work in more detail in the next chapter, but it is always worthwhile for the guest to spend a little time in the deer larder just to see exactly how well he placed his bullet. The knowledge may help to ensure that a mistake, if any, is not repeated in the future.

Finally, we might consider the practice of tipping the stalker after a visit to the hill. Stalking as a profession is not at all well paid, even though a house and perhaps a vehicle of some kind are included with the job. The antlers and tusks of the stags and the tusks of the hinds are usually considered to be part of a stalker's perks, and it is normal for the guests to show their appreciation by making some form of financial contribution. There is no 'correct' amount; the size of the tip will depend on the local 'norm' as well as the generosity of the guest. It should

If there is no burn nearby a handful of sphagnum moss will serve quite well to clean your knife, and hands, after the gralloch.

A very poor head, and a beast that would certainly be considered suitable for culling.

also, of course, reflect on how well and obligingly the stalker has done his job. A tip, after all, shows the guests' appreciation of a job well done; it is not a fixed charge to be met whether or not the stalker has made any real effort to make your day enjoyable and successful. However, if you decide to retain the antlers as a trophy, then it is only fair to make up the value of these in addition to any tip you may decide to leave. The guest who goes home with £15 worth of antlers while leaving behind a £5 tip will not be top of any stalker's popularity poll.

10

Larder Work

Most of the work that I am including under the general heading of 'Larder Work' will, in fact, be done by the stalker, or by an under-stalker or ghillie. However, there is no reason why any stalker, experienced or novice, amateur or professional, should not be at least familiar with the general idea of what must be done with a carcase once it has been taken off the hill. There may be a time when, for one reason or another, you are left to cope with a beast without professional assistance, and provided you have an idea of what is required there is no reason why you should not make an acceptable job of it.

The exact method in which a beast is handled in the larder will vary from one forest to another depending on what is the normal practice for that particular estate, or the manner in which the stalker was trained originally. Some game dealers have different requirements of the carcases they collect to others and it is likely that these requirements will become increasingly stringent as new rules and regulations are brought in to deal with the handling of meat for human consumption. In general though, the aim is to clean the carcase, allow free circulation of air around and through it and to identify the pluck (the heart, lungs and liver), so that it may be subjected to veterinary inspection at a later stage in its journey to the consumer.

The first thing to be done when a carcase reaches the larder is usually to weigh it. Stag and hind weights are normally recorded with the head and feet on, pluck still inside, but gralloch removed. Some estates may follow a different practice, weighing clean, i.e. after the heart, lungs and liver have been removed, or even taking the weight after the head and feet are off, but larder weight is usually taken as the weight of the beast as it was brought in from the hill. There should be some form of weighing machine – a balance bar, spring balance or set of scales to weigh your beast on – and the weight is usually recorded in stone and pounds.

Most larders will have some form of mechanical handling aid – probably a rope and pulley system – to help you hoist the stag up off the floor. If you are weighing it on a spring balance, then hook the point of the balance firmly between two ribs, attach the other end to the pulley system and hoist away. Once you have noted the weight then the beast can be lowered down again ready to work on.

Some stalkers work on the floor of the larder, but the job is much easier if a bench is used to bring the carcase to a comfortable working height. A simple bench, about three feet long by one foot wide, with six-inch high boards along each of the long sides will hold a stag or hind quite comfortably and greatly simplify the work. Lower your carcase so that it is lying on its back on the bench

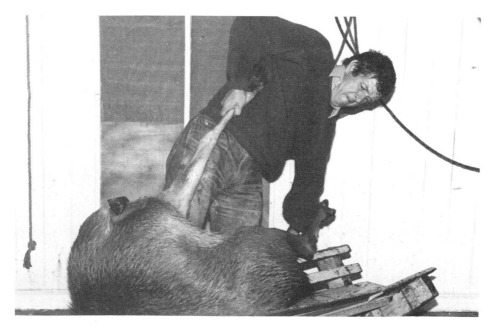

Skinning a beast. Begin by lifting the beast up on to the workbench.

with the feet sticking up into the air and the head and neck hanging down over one end of the bench. You now require a sharp knife, a saw, a spreader (a piece of wood about six inches long, notched at either end) for the chest and a gambrel to hang the beast from when you have finished work.

Begin by removing the lower legs and feet. Take each limb in turn and cut round with your knife just where the joint bends. Then hold the foot in one hand and brace the joint across the other forearm. A quick snap backwards against the natural bend of the joint, then a tidying up with the knife should remove the lower legs cleanly and neatly. When you are removing the back legs, make a slit between the bone and the Achilles tendon; this will be used later to hook over the ends of the gambrel when hanging the beast up.

While you are at the rear end of the carcase, spread the legs wide apart and cut down through the flesh between the legs until you reach the pelvic bone. If you are dealing with a hind which has been suckling a calf then cut the udder away from either side of the gralloching cut as the milk will quickly go sour and taint the carcase if left. Then take the saw and make a cut through the pelvis where you have exposed the bone with your knife. Cut around the vent with the knife and remove what is left of the bowel from the carcase, taking care not to spill any of the contents into the body cavity.

Go round to the front end and make a cut through the neck skin from the throat to the rear end of the breast bone. Cut down the length of the breast bone with the knife, making sure that you are cutting exactly down the centre, then complete the cut using the saw. Keep sawing until the two halves of the rib cage can be sprung apart. Now take the spreader and force the two sides of the rib cage open, inserting the spreader to hold them apart. There will be several bits of tissue joining the heart and lungs to the rib cage; cut these away with the knife, then cut away the diaphragm where it joins the ribs, following the edge right down to the centre of the spine.

At this point, some stalkers will leave the kidneys in the carcase, some remove them with the rest of the pluck. If taking the kidneys out, ease each one away from the body, complete with its coating of fat, then cut through the main blood vessel which runs along the spine, severing it just behind the liver. Take care not to damage the fillet when doing this. Hold the liver, and lift the complete pluck up and forwards, cutting the main blood vessel away from the spine as you find necessary. There will probably still be quite a lot of blood left in the body cavity and this may obscure your view to some extent. Once the pluck is clear of the chest cavity it can be removed completely by cutting down on either side of the windpipe, then severing the windpipe at the throat, or it can be left attached to the carcase by the windpipe.

Next, fit your gambrel through the slits behind the Achilles tendons, attach it to the pulley hook and hoist the carcase up to hang and cool. As the weight comes off the bench and the carcase hangs vertically, head downwards, the remaining blood will splash out of the chest cavity. Tie off the hoist, take a hose pipe and give the body cavity a gentle but thorough wash out, remove all surplus body fat to speed cooling, then tag the carcase and its pluck (if a tagging system is in operation on the forest).

The head will also have to be removed, but if the carcase is left to hang overnight with the head attached the extra weight will help to stretch out the beast and thus produce a better looking carcase. Finally, give the larder floor and walls a good wash down, clean the knife and saw, wash your own hands and go and record the details in the game book. The deer which are sent away to game dealers or to venison processing plants are normally required to travel in their skins, since the skin helps to protect the carcase while in transit. However, if you want a beast for your own consumption then the normal practice is to skin it when it first comes in from the hill then hang it for whatever time you consider necessary to improve the texture and flavour.

Like the rest of the larder work, skinning would normally be the prerogative of the stalker, but there is nothing particularly difficult in skinning a beast, and no reason why you should not do it yourself if the need arises. The methods which are used will vary from one person to another, but I will describe the method which we use ourselves. It works well enough and you can always alter it to suit yourself if you wish to do so.

It is possible to skin a beast on the larder floor, but it is more convenient and more hygienic to use some form of bench. The same bench as is used for the normal handling of carcases in the larder will work quite adequately, or a special skinning bench can be constructed. We have one in our own larder. The main difference between it and the normal bench is that the skinning bench, at about two feet six inches high, is some six inches lower than the other, and the working surface is about eighteen inches wide instead of a foot. If you are only going to be

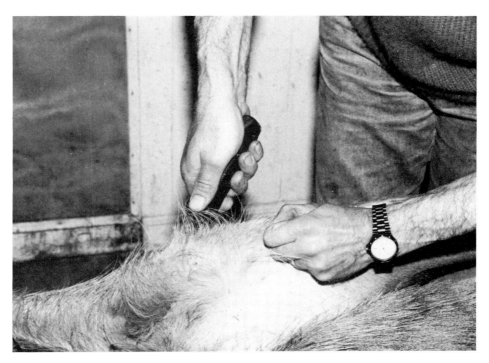

Slit up the skin of the hind legs, sharp edge of the blade outwards.

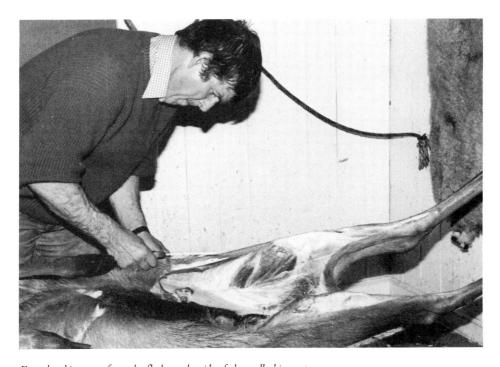

Ease the skin away from the flesh on the side of the gralloching cut.

149

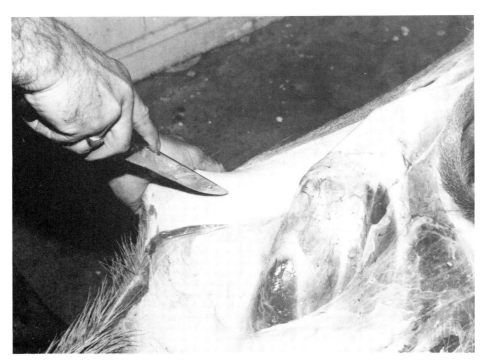

Keep the knife point well back from where the flesh and hide appear to be joined.

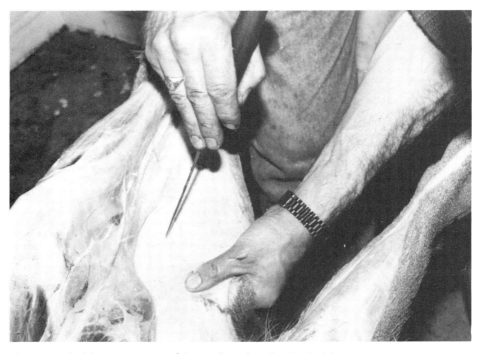

Skinning one hind leg. Note position of the initial cut along the other hind leg.

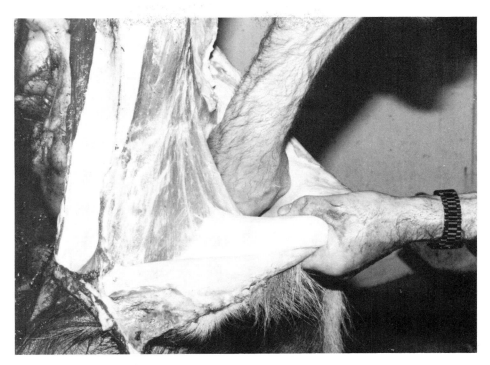

The stag is hoisted up to a convenient working height to allow the vent to be removed.

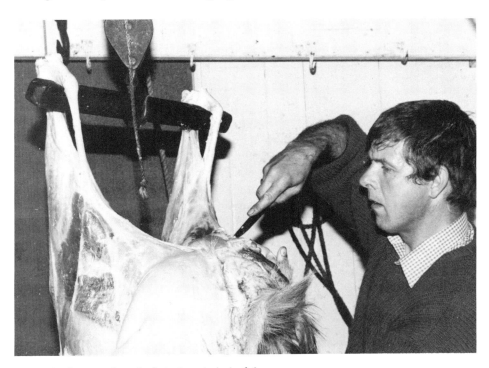

Fisting the skin away from the flesh along the back of the carcase.

151

A steady pull will take the hide away right along the back.

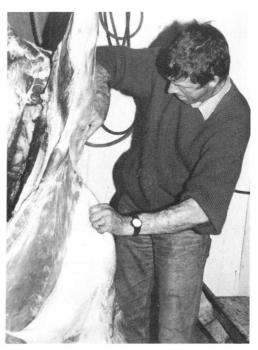

skinning an occasional beast then it is hardly worth the trouble of making a special bench, and your normal larder bench should be perfectly adequate.

Begin by weighing your carcase, then lowering it on to the bench, feet up, just as with a beast for the game dealer. Cut through the skin of the lower leg on each limb in turn, then put the point of the knife under the skin, sharp edge outwards, and slit the skin along the length of the leg and on as far as the gralloch cut (with the hind legs) or the centre of the chest (with the front legs). Take the skin along each side of the gralloch cut in turn and begin to work the hide away from the flesh. The hide is quite tightly joined to the underlying meat in this area, and you will probably need to use the tip of your knife to ease the two apart. (It helps if the knife is not too sharp when performing this operation, especially if you are planning to cure the hide to make a rug.) If you draw the tip of the knife gently along a few inches above where the hide and the flesh appear to be joined and ease them apart with the other hand at the same time then they should separate without damaging the thin underlayers of skin – an important point in producing a good looking carcase, though it will make little difference to the quality of the meat.

Keep gently easing off the hide on either side of the belly and on the hind legs until the sides of the bench start to interfere with your work. Then slit behind the Achilles tendons, insert a gambrel and hoist the carcase up a little way into the air. This should clear you to skin around the rump and right down the hind legs, removing the lower legs as you go. The actual separation of hide and flesh will become easier at this point, and you will find that you are able to fist the two

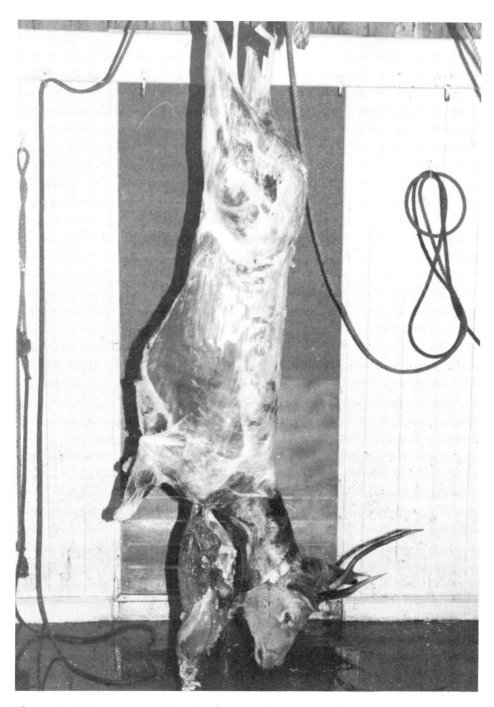

The completed job – a young stag skinned out for the deep freeze. The head is left on for a day to help stretch out the carcase.

apart without using the knife at all, still taking care to leave the under-skin intact.

As you progress, keep heightening the carcase to bring your work to a comfortable level. The whole of the hide from the back should come away with a steady pull, but beware as you reach the shoulders, as the flesh here is very easily ripped. A little gentle fisting around the shoulders and in the 'armpits' should clear the hide here. Skin the forelegs and remove the lower limbs, then a last satisfying rip ought to bring operations as far as the top of the neck. Cut the hide away just behind the ears, then dress the carcase out just as you would for a normal beast. Cut the pelvic girdle, remove the back passage, remove the pluck and body fat, then wash down. If there are any warble grubs showing in the back of the carcase, remove these by pressing the flat of the knife blade against the edge of the hole. Leave it to hang for twenty-four hours, then take off the head. The carcase can then be left to hang until the meat is ready for butchering.

The question of how long a carcase should hang before it is ready to eat is really a matter of personal choice. The texture of the meat will, in any case, vary with the age and condition of the animal when it was killed, and the length of hanging time must be adjusted in accordance with the weather. In general, though, the longer a carcase is allowed to hang, the tenderer and tastier the meat will be.

In summer, if the weather is warm, or worse, muggy and thundery, then a week might be more than long enough to hang the beast. In winter, a fortnight would be about the norm, and perhaps as long as a month for an old beast in cold weather. Do not be guided by appearances when assessing the carcase – the outer skin will go black and leathery in a very short time. The most reliable test is to use your nose, and smell for any hint of the meat going off, particularly along the neck and around the kidney area. As soon as the meat smells anything less than fresh, the time is coming to think about butchering the carcase. Of course, if you prefer your meat chewy, then cut it up sooner – the day after you shoot it if you wish. It will still be edible, but you may need sharp teeth and a strong jaw to cope with it.

Butchery is a very skilled trade, and a trained butcher's cutter will make a far better job of jointing a carcase than will an amateur. However, there is no reason why the amateur stalker should not be his own butcher as well, and there is no real problem in making a perfectly acceptable job of a carcase.

You need a place to work (a big kitchen table will serve very well), a chopping board to work on, at least one good, sharp knife, a meat saw (or a clean hacksaw) and a cleaver, or the chopper out of the wood shed, well scrubbed down for the occasion. If you have two knives – a boning knife with a narrow blade about four to six inches long, and a longer, stiffer butchering knife, then so much the better. A steel, to keep the knives properly sharpened, polythene bags to freeze the joints in and a dog or two to catch the scraps, and you are ready to begin. As before, I will describe the way I cut up a hind or stag: it isn't necessarily the right way or the best way, and it certainly isn't the only way, but it works for me so it should also work for you.

You can start in one of two ways. The proper way is to saw the carcase in half

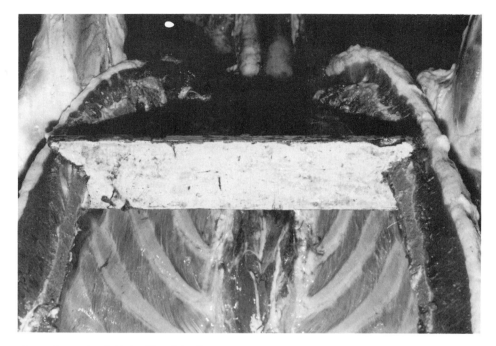

A spreader, used to hold the sides of the chest apart.

along the backbone, then butcher the halves one at a time, but it can be quite tricky to cut cleanly down the full length of the spine. If you prefer not to try this then you can cut the carcase into three sections laterally, then split each in turn. The end result should be just the same. Take the neck off where it joins the shoulders and chop it into sections for stock or stew. If the beast was neck shot then there will be a damaged section that is best discarded or used for dog meat. Count back five ribs from the front and cut off the shoulder. This can be left whole as a single joint; it looks very impressive but is a swine to carve. I usually prefer to bone the shoulder out and roll it; it is then easier to cook and carve, though a little harder to butcher.

To bone a shoulder, first remove the rib cage. Take your boning knife and score down on either side of each rib on the inside of the joint. Then, starting at the breast bone, work down each rib in turn, cutting the meat away from the bone. You may find it easiest to do a little bit of each rib in turn, gradually working down until you reach the spine. Take special care here to clean all the meat off the bone, and the rib cage will come away, to be chopped up for stock, or used as spare ribs. Next follow the line of the shoulder blade with your boning knife, then cut the flesh away above and beneath the blade, keeping as close to the bone as possible. Raise the shoulder blade and twist it, then cut away the sinews which attach it to the leg bone. Remove the lower leg at the elbow joint, then cut out the upper leg bone and the joint is ready to be rolled and frozen or cooked.

Next cut the ribs and loin away somewhere about the top of the haunch. There will be a couple of strips of hard, dry meat that was the animal's belly; this can be minced or used for stock, or, of course, fed to the dogs. Chop away the ends of the ribs above where the edible meat finishes, then separate the ribs into chops, cutting down with the knife and splitting off each chop with the cleaver. The section from the last rib back to where you separated the loin from the haunch can be left as a single joint or cut up into loin chops.

This should leave you with the haunches. If you wish, these can be left as a single joint, and will feed a small army. Alternatively the haunches can be divided into as many smaller joints as you wish – two, three, or four good-sized joints can be taken from a single haunch. If you like venison steaks then you can start in at one end of the haunch and cut as many slices of steak as you think you will use, the whole haunch if you wish. If you are going to cut a lot of steaks it is worth the bother of boning out the haunch first; if only a few then it is easier to work around the bone.

Once the whole carcase is jointed it will take up surprisingly little space, though you may be left with quite a large pile of bits of bone, fat and hard skin. We boil all the scraps up for the dogs, but then we have rather a lot of dogs. If you have only the odd dog, or none, and are more frugal than ourselves, then the odds and ends can be used for stock, venison burgers and spare ribs. Butchering is actually a lot easier than it may sound. Most of it is common sense, and if you do cut in the wrong place no real harm is done, provided it isn't yourself or your assistant on the receiving end.

One other job that you may wish to do in the larder is to take the antlers of a stag for a trophy. First remove the head from the carcase. Cut across just behind the ears, then follow round under the chin. Locate the point at which the neck joins the skull (the atlas joint) and cut through the sinews on either side. Take hold of the antlers and twist the head sideways, and the joint will open enough for you to complete the separation of head from neck.

Skin the head. This is harder than it sounds actually, since the antlers get in the way at every opportunity. The best way is to start under the chin, cutting from throat to chin, then work around from one side of the head to another. The worst bits are around the pedicles, but since there is no requirement to produce a show piece you can hack away until the skin finally surrenders without doing any damage. Once you have all the hide removed, take a saw and try to visualise the line you want to follow. This should be from below the pedicles and through the tops of the eye sockets, meeting either side in the middle of the nose. Make certain that you are cutting evenly if you have to work from each side rather than making a single cut right through. Eventually the top of the skull (with antlers attached), should come neatly away from the rest of the head.

The skull now needs to be boiled to remove the remaining bits of meat and tissue, then scraped and scrubbed clean. The longer you boil it the easier it is to clean the last few particles of tissue away, but beware! If you over-cook the skull, the bones may separate into their component parts. A couple of hours gentle boiling should be enough. There will be a number of little bits of very thin bone in the top of the nostril; these too can be scraped out. Then the head is ready to be mounted on a board and hung on your wall. If you think it may spoil your appetite to look at the headgear of the donor when eating your venison, then don't hang him in the dining room. I will look at ways of cooking venison in the next chapter.

11

Venison Cookery

In the previous chapters I have tried to give some of the flavour of a day on the hill, as well as looking at the equipment the stalker will require and the methods he will use to conclude a successful stalk. For many stalkers the end product of a day is a beast hung in the larder which the game dealer will call to take away in due course. For others, more discerning perhaps, the true conclusion of a day on the hill is a roast haunch of venison carved into succulent slices and served with game chips, carrots, peas and rowan jelly. Those stalkers will need no persuading of the merits of venison on the table. It is to the others, and to all those who have never sampled the finest and healthiest meat available in Britain today, that I am addressing this section. This is the chapter that will deal with the flavour of stalking in the literal sense.

There are few meats that can approach venison for flavour and none that can

The cook feeding up a future customer. Very few stags will ever approach this close to a human, except in times of extreme hunger.

Hind and calf, feeding in mid-winter.

match it for healthy eating. The red deer spend all their lives out on the open hill, eating only pure, natural food. They stay lean and healthy by leading an active life, building strong muscle but laying down very little fat. In consequence, the fat content of wild venison is lower than that of almost any other meat. The slow growth rate of wild deer means that the meat is close textured and fine grained, with real flavour and, of course, there are no growth promoters, no antibiotics, no flavour enhancers, no tenderisers and no water added to 'improve' the product. Venison is just good, lean, healthy and tasty meat.

Compare the life of a red deer with that of a broiler chicken. The chicken will live the whole of its short life in a completely false environment, lit, heated and ventilated at the whim of the poultryman. It will be vaccinated against a whole range of diseases – fowl pest, infectious bronchitis, and gumboro disease spring quickly to mind. It will be fed antibiotics in its food as a matter of course, and probably some sort of arsenical compound as a growth promoter. It will be slaughtered at six or seven weeks old and frozen in a plastic bag within an hour of being killed. Between being killed and being frozen it will have been injected with a mixture of water and polyphosphate up to 20 per cent of its live weight. We will cook it and eat it, and wonder why food has no real flavour these days. It is just as well we can't taste all the chemical residues left in the flesh of chicken.

The deer will have lived its life out in the open, eating only what vegetation it can find on the hill, uncontaminated by any of the chemicals that are fed to, sprayed over or injected into the broiler chicken. Its growth will be slower and the beast may be several years old when it is shot – old enough for its flesh to have developed both texture and flavour. After being killed, the venison should have been allowed to hang in a cool larder and develop more flavour, not pumped full

159

Stags in velvet, just beginning to shed their winter coats.

Antlers are useful for scratching those awkward spots that can't be reached any other way.

A yeld hind – an ideal beast for the kitchen.

of water and phosphates, then frozen within minutes of death. The broiler industry certainly provides the housewife with cheap meat, in considerable quantities, but the quality of that meat can bear no comparison with a good haunch or shoulder of Highland venison.

If venison is such good meat, why is it not more widely available in the shops? And why is it so expensive when it is on the butcher's counter? Good questions, and not so easily answered. Availability probably reflects demand. If more customers asked for venison, then more butchers and supermarket chains would begin to stock it. And if more outlets stocked venison, more people could try it and discover for themselves just how good it can be. The answer to the first question then is to go along to your butcher and ask him to get some venison in for you (assuming that you haven't been thoughtful enough to bring a beast home after your stalking trip). If your butcher can't, or won't, order venison for you, then look for one who can and will. That should take care of availability. Now we have to consider price.

Venison prices as paid to stalking estates vary greatly from season to season. In recent years they have been as high as 95p per pound, and as low as 45p per pound. That is per pound, dead weight, including the hide. Skinned and jointed, that same venison can cost up to ten times as much from your butcher and I, for one, can't explain the reason why. You might like to make your own enquiries at the same time as ordering your joint. If enough people do, then the price might drop, and the demand might rise as well. Alternatively, buy a haunch, or a shoulder, or better still a whole beast, and take it home for your freezer after your stalking holiday. That way you should get it at wholesale price and know it has been properly hung as well.

So how about cooking venison? There is nothing intrinsically difficult about venison cookery. If you can cook beef or lamb, then you can cook venison. There are one or two pitfalls to avoid – venison can be tough and it can be dry – but properly handled, it should be neither of these. Toughness can be avoided by proper hanging and slow cooking; dryness can be prevented by larding with fat, cooking in tinfoil or marinading prior to cooking. There are plenty of exotic ways of preparing venison, but to my mind none of them can compare with a good, old-fashioned roast haunch, so let us begin with that.

Roast Haunch of Venison

If there is a problem with venison for the table it is that there is a tendency for joints to be rather dry. This is because there is such a low fat content in wild venison – an excellent thing from a health viewpoint, but a potential problem when cooking. Marinading is excellent for adding flavours to the meat, but if a juicy, tender joint with the full flavour of venison is what you require, then this should serve your needs with very little trouble.

Pre-heat the oven to a high temperature (gas mark 6/200°C/400°F). Put your haunch into a roasting tin, add some red wine and a generous knob of butter, then cover joint and tin with baking foil before putting it into the oven. After about half an hour, when the juices have been sealed into the meat, turn the oven down to gas mark 4/180°C/350°F, then roast for 25 minutes per pound, plus 25 minutes, basting from time to time. Remove the baking foil about 20 minutes before the end of cooking to allow the meat to brown. This assumes that you are cooking a properly hung joint. If the meat has not been hung, or if you are unsure what treatment it had before coming into your hands, then it might be safer to alter the cooking method slightly.

Start with a hot oven as before (gas mark 6/200°C/400°/F), but drop the temperature to gas mark 3/170°C/325°F and allow 30 minutes per pound plus 30 minutes. If you want a really melt-in-the-mouth tenderness from your joint, then you might like to follow the example of one friend of mine who roasted a whole haunch, about fourteen pounds weight, for 12 hours in a very slow oven, basting every half hour. It was delicious, but also a lot of work. However, if you are faced with a potentially tough joint, and have the time to spare, then such treatment should virtually guarantee a tender result.

Stuffed Shoulder of Venison

A whole shoulder can be treated in much the same way as a haunch, roasted slowly in baking foil, and will look very impressive on the table. Unfortunately, there is far less meat on a shoulder than might appear at first glance, and carving a shoulder on the bone is a task for the expert. Wherever you cut you will find a bone lurking just beneath the surface. It is far better to bone out the shoulder when butchering the carcase, or get your butcher to bone it when you buy it, and roast it with a stuffing inside. Then it can be sliced off in chunks, and will go much further than the same meat on the bone.

The procedure for roasting the joint is the same as for a haunch – butter and red wine, a baking foil coat and a nice steady oven. Shoulder meat is slightly tougher than haunch, so slow roasting is perhaps more important with this joint. The main difference is in the initial preparation and the choice of ingredients used to make the stuffing. Any type of stuffing you fancy can be used, though obviously some will go better with venison than others. If you don't have a particular favourite of your own then try a shoulder stuffed with one of our favourite mixtures.

Pâté and Mushroom

Fry chopped onion and mushrooms in butter until soft. Mix up some liver pâté, add the onions and mushrooms, a few spoonfuls of cream and salt and pepper.

Herby Sausagemeat

Pork sausagemeat, breadcrumbs, thyme, sage, parsley, onion, beaten egg, salt and pepper. Fry the onion, then mix all ingredients thoroughly.

Carrot, Ham and Mushroom

Fry chopped onion in butter. Add diced ham, chopped carrots, mushrooms, and a little port and cook for a few more minutes. Add breadcrumbs, parsley, salt and pepper, plus a little beaten egg to bind.

Having prepared the stuffing, open out the shoulder and spread the stuffing over it. Re-roll the shoulder and tie it into shape, or sew it with needle and thread. If all the stuffing won't fit into the joint then cook it separately and serve with the joint. The quantity you require will obviously vary with the size of the joint you are preparing, and the proportions of the ingredients should be juggled to suit your own taste. Stuffed shoulder is also excellent served cold with a salad, or in sandwiches.

Civet of Venison

This is a superb venison stew, and can be prepared with raw meat, or with the leftovers from a joint. It cooks in a rich, thick gravy and has a delightful aroma that will fill the kitchen as it stews.

Ingredients

2lb venison (cooked or raw) cut into chunks
2oz flour
1 pint stock
2 onions, chopped
1 clove garlic
1 tablespoon wine vinegar
1 glass red wine
parsley
½lb mushrooms, sliced
salt and pepper to taste

Method

Begin by gently frying the onions and garlic in a little fat until they are soft but not browned. Remove from pan. Then, if using raw meat, coat it in seasoned flour and fry it until it browns (add a little more fat if necessary). Return the onions and garlic to the pan, add a little stock, stirring gently, add the wine, the wine vinegar and cover with stock, then bring to the boil. Add the parsley then cover the pan and cook in a slow oven for 2 to 3 hours. Add the mushrooms about half an hour before serving. If the meat is already cooked, then omit the frying stage, and reduce the cooking time to 1½ or 2 hours. As with most stews, the flavour will be greatly improved if the civet is cooked, then left to stand for a few hours, or overnight, then re-heated for serving at gas mark 4/180°C/350°F for about an hour.

Venison Wellington

This is a great dish for a dinner party, looking as good as it tastes. We make it with fillet of venison, making sure that all the bits of gristle and fat are removed before cooking, but any good lean cut would be suitable. If you use shoulder meat then it will need a little longer pre-cooking to ensure that it will be tender. It is quite a filling dish; three pounds of meat would serve at least 8 hungry people. The ingredients are all approximate; you can juggle them to suit your own tastes.

Ingredients

3lb venison fillet
6oz mushrooms, sliced
4oz onions
1oz butter
8oz liver pâté
4 tablespoons fresh cream
1 egg, beaten
salt and pepper
1 packet puff pastry

Method

Trim any bits of fat or gristle off the meat, brush it with a little oil, sprinkle some salt and pepper over it, wrap it in baking foil and pre-cook it for about half an hour in an oven at gas mark 7/220°C/425°F. Take it out of the oven and allow it to cool. While the meat is cooking, slice the mushrooms and onions and fry them in butter until soft. Mash the pâté and then stir in the onions, mushrooms and cream, seasoning to taste. Roll the pastry out, place the venison fillets on the pastry and spread them over with the filling. Brush the edges of the pastry with the beaten egg, then wrap the pastry round the meat as if wrapping a parcel. Use any trimmings from the pastry to decorate the parcel, lay the whole thing on a baking sheet and brush over with beaten egg. Cook in the oven for 30 to 40 minutes, or until the pastry is golden brown and well risen.

ACCOMPANIMENTS

Rowan Jelly

As cranberry sauce goes with turkey, mint sauce with lamb and horseradish sauce with beef, so rowan jelly is the proper and fitting accompaniment to roast venison. The rowan tree or mountain ash thrives on the hills and valleys where the red deer is found, and in the autumn, the orange red clusters of fruits blaze out like decorations on a Christmas tree. The fruits themselves are too bitter to eat (for humans – birds love them in spite of their taste), but will make a delightfully tart jelly that complements and enhances the taste of venison. It also goes well with mutton, grouse and pheasant.

Ingredients

4lb rowan berries
4lb crab apples (or cooking apples)
6 pints water
castor sugar (the amount depends on how much juice is left after cooking)

Method

Wash and stalk the berries and wash the apples. Use the crab apples whole, but if using cooking apples, cut them into chunks. Put the fruit in a saucepan, add the water and bring to the boil. Cover the pan and simmer for 20 to 25 minutes until the fruit is tender. Strain the fruit and liquid through a jelly bag (we began with a clean pillowcase) and leave until it stops dripping. *Do not* squeeze the bag; if you do, the jelly will be cloudy. Measure the liquid and weigh out 1lb sugar for each pint of juice. Put the sugar in a dish and warm it in a low oven, (gas mark ¼/110°C/225°F) for about 10 minutes. Warm the juice, stir in the sugar and bring to the boil. Boil for 10 minutes or so until the setting point is reached, skim if necessary, then pot and seal it. The finished jelly is a glorious deep orange red colour, not unlike the fruit from which it is made.

Brown Lentils

Lentils cooked in this way may not look particularly good, but their looks are deceiving. Try them once, and I guarantee you will keep coming back for more.

Ingredients

8oz brown lentils
olive oil or butter
1 onion, finely chopped
1 carrot, peeled and diced
2 cloves garlic, chopped
stock
salt and pepper to taste

Method

Rinse the lentils and drain them. Heat the oil or butter in a pan and fry the onion, carrot and garlic for a few minutes. Add the lentils, cover with stock, season with salt and pepper, then bring to the boil, cover and simmer for about an hour. When nearly all the stock has been absorbed and the lentils are tender, turn the lentils into a serving dish, dot them with a little butter and serve.

Cumberland Sauce

This is a delightfully spicy sauce which we sometimes use instead of rowan jelly to accompany venison, or indeed any other roast meat and game. The citrus fruits give it a tangy bite. It can be served hot or kept in a refrigerator and served cold. Either way it is delicious. It is supposed to keep for a couple of months in a closed jar in the fridge, but ours rarely survives a second day.

Ingredients

1lb redcurrant jelly
½ bottle port
1 orange
1 lemon
¼ teaspoon cayenne pepper
2 tablespoons Worcestershire sauce

Method

Put the redcurrant jelly and the port in a saucepan and bring to the boil, stirring from time to time. Simmer until the liquid is reduced by about a third. Add in the grated rind and juice of the orange and the lemon, the cayenne pepper, the Worcestershire sauce and stir well. Serve hot with roast venison, or allow to cool for use with cold meats.

12
Stalking and the Law

There is obviously a moral as well as a legal obligation on any sportsman to ensure that he complies with the law when pursuing his chosen sport. This is particularly important at the moment, when the opponents of field sports will seize any opportunity to attack those who quite legitimately choose to shoot, fish, hunt and stalk. The 'anti' lobby is both vociferous and well organised, and can cause more than enough trouble without the aid of sportsmen scoring 'own goals' by breaking the law, whether by accident or design. There is not really a great deal for the stalker to do to ensure that he complies with the existing legislation, and it is the responsibility of everyone who stalks, or shoots, hunts or fishes, to ensure that they stay within the legislation.

There are two main areas in which the stalker is required to comply with the law. One relates to the deer – the type of weapon which may be used, close seasons, times when shooting is permitted – and the other, to the stalker himself – the need for Game Licences and Firearm Certificates. There is also a very considerable body of legislation concerned with poaching, but this should not concern the legitimate stalker. Additionally, there are regulations concerning the sale of venison, which may be of interest to the stalker but are not directly concerned with stalking for sport.

The law in Scotland is often different from English Law, though not invariably so. Some Acts of Parliament apply to both England and Wales, and Scotland; some Acts are specifically designated to apply only in Scotland. In a book concerned with Highland deer stalking it is obviously Scots Law that is relevant, but where there are major differences, such as with close seasons, I have included a summary of English as well as Scottish regulations.

CLOSE SEASONS

In Scotland, close seasons are set by the Deer (Scotland) Act, 1959 (amended by the Deer (Amendment) (Scotland) Act, 1982), as is much of the legislation concerning stalkers. The close season for red deer is between 21 October and 30 June for stags, and 16 February and 20 October for hinds. This means that stags may be killed between 1 July and 20 October, while hinds may be shot between 21 October and 15 February. In England and Wales, the close season runs from 1 May to 31 July for stags, and from 1 March to 31 October for hinds.

There are some exceptions to the close season which are permitted primarily in order to prevent damage to woodland and farm land by marauding deer.

167

A red deer hind. The hind stalking season in Scotland runs from 21 October to 15 February.

These exceptions are intended to protect trees and crops, not to provide a loophole which will allow an extension to the stalking season. Stalking for sport should take place only during the permitted season, and the control of marauding deer left to the occupier of the land and his employees. Indeed, any other person killing deer during the close season must be authorised by the Red Deer Commission.

NIGHT SHOOTING

As far as the sporting stalker is concerned, night shooting of deer is illegal. For this purpose night is defined as the period between one hour after sunset and one hour before sunrise. Again, there are certain exceptions to these rules, designed to allow the protection of crops by the occupiers of agricultural land, but these do not apply to the sport of stalking.

RIFLES AND AMMUNITION

As is the case with close seasons, different legislation covers the legal requirements for rifles and ammunition to be used against deer in Scotland and in England and Wales. South of the border, the Schedule 2 Deer Act, 1963 applies,

Red deer stag. The season for stalking stags in Scotland is from 1 July to 20 October.

while in Scotland the regulations are laid down in the Deer (Firearms) (Scotland) Order, 1985. The main difference between the two sets of legislation is the way in which they define a legal weapon. The English and Welsh law specifies the calibre of rifle which may be used as well as the minimum muzzle energy, whereas the Scottish legislation says nothing about calibre, but defines a minimum performance for the ammunition used. Most rifle and ammunition combinations which are legal under one system will be legal under the other, but there are exceptions. These are generally more applicable to roe stalkers.

Scotland

The law requires that three criteria are met –

bullet – not less than 100 grains
muzzle velocity – not less than 2,450 feet per second
muzzle energy – not less than 1,750 foot pounds

Note that all three requirements must be met in order for the ammunition to be legal for use against all types of deer. In addition, the bullet must be an expanding type, designed to deform in a predictable manner. The Order also makes special provision for ammunition to be used against roe deer.

bullet – not less than 50 grains
muzzle velocity – not less than 2,450 feet per second
muzzle energy – not less than 1,000 foot pounds

It is important to realise that certain rifles which are legal for use against roe in Scotland are not legal for use against red deer, and that they are not legal against any species in England or Wales. This would apply to such calibres as the .222 and .223 Remington, the .220 Swift and the .224 Weatherby Magnum. While these would never be legal against any species of deer in England or Wales they are legal for roe in Scotland and, in theory, would also be legal for red deer, provided that ammunition were available that met the triple requirements of a bullet of 100 grains or more, muzzle velocity of 2,450 feet per second or more and muzzle energy of 1,750 foot pounds or more. They would still be illegal against all species in England and Wales.

England and Wales

It is illegal to shoot deer with a rifle that does not meet the minimum specifications for calibre and muzzle energy –

rifle – calibre of not less than .240 inches
muzzle energy – not less than 1,700 foot pounds

In addition, the bullet must be soft-nosed or hollow-nosed.

It is possible, in theory at any rate, to have a rifle that would be legal for use against red deer in England and Wales, but illegal in Scotland, as well as one that would reverse this and be legal in Scotland but illegal in England and Wales. In practice, any rifle with a calibre greater than .240, which is legal under one set of requirements should also be legal under the other. It is important to note, however, that certain calibres can be legal with some ammunition and illegal with others. For example, the .243 with an 80-grain bullet is illegal against red deer in Scotland, but legal against roe, and against red deer in England. Several types of ammunition fail to meet the muzzle velocity requirements in Scotland (the .30-30 with 150-grain bullet, .30-06 with 220-grain bullet and .303 with 215-grain bullet), but will satisfy the requirements of English Law. A change of ammunition may mean that the rifle becomes legal again – the .30-06 with 110-, 150- or 180-grain bullet satisfies Scottish regulations, as does the .303 with 150-or 180-grain bullet. If in doubt, consult the ammunition manufacturer, or your local gun dealer. Data about the performance of a particular make of ammunition is often supplied on the side of the packet.

SHOTGUNS

Under certain circumstances, it is permissible to use a shotgun against deer, but only on arable or enclosed land, by the occupier or by certain other specified persons, and only when necessary to prevent serious damage to crops, trees, or

Stags cooling off in a loch during the close season.

foodstuffs. If a shotgun is so used, it must have a gauge of not less than 12-bore, and fire a single, rifled, non-spherical slug of not less than 380 grains, or a cartridge loaded with SSG or larger shot. The minimum shot size for roe deer is AAA or larger. Again, these provisions are made to allow the control of marauding deer on agricultural land or in gardens, and should not concern the sporting stalker unless he is asked to assist in such control.

OTHER WEAPONS

It is illegal to use weapons such as longbows, crossbows, spears and air weapons to kill deer. The legislation makes it an offence to kill or injure deer by any means other than shooting. This would include snares, poisons and dogs as well as weapons such as those listed above.

OTHER METHODS

The legislation also prohibits certain methods of pursuing deer. It is, for example, illegal to shoot at deer from an aircraft. Of more concern to the stalker, perhaps, is the part of the legislation which prohibits the use of a vehicle to drive deer on unenclosed land with the intention of taking, killing or injuring them. This presumably makes it illegal to 'stalk' directly from an all-terrain vehicle if the deer are moved ('driven') in the course of the stalk.

GAME LICENCES

Anyone wishing to stalk and kill deer on unenclosed land should be the holder of a valid Game Licence. This can be obtained from a Post Office on payment of a small fee, and can be obtained for various different periods. A normal licence will run from the time it is taken out until 31 July following, i.e. one issued on 1 August would run for a full year, one issued on 30 July would run for only one day. In addition, a licence may be taken out to run from the time of issue (after 31 July) until 31 October the same year, or from the time of issue (after 31 October) until 31 July following, or for any continuous period of fourteen days. In practice, almost everybody would simply take out a full licence which covers the shooting of game birds and hares as well as deer. There are a few exceptions, however – holders of a gamekeeper's licence on their employer's land, members of the Royal Family and gamekeepers on Crown lands – but in general, if you are going stalking you should have a Game Licence.

FIREARMS CERTIFICATES

Anyone wishing to possess, acquire or use a firearm, other than a shotgun or airgun, must first obtain a Firearm Certificate from their local Chief Officer of Police. It would appear therefore, that before the novice can take up deer stalking he must first hold a firearm certificate. However, in practice this is not the case. Most beginners to stalking, and indeed, many experienced stalkers, make use of the professional stalker's rifle, or an estate rifle, and do not hold a certificate at all.

This has been the general practice for many years, though prior to the Firearms (Amendment) Act, 1988, borrowing a rifle in such a way was not strictly within the.letter of the law. The 1988 act permits a person of or over the age of 17 years to borrow a rifle from the occupier of private premises and use it on those premises, in the presence of either the occupier or the occupier's servant, without holding a Firearm Certificate. Therefore, in practice, the novice stalker has no need for a Certificate unless he wishes to obtain his own rifle, or to purchase ammunition.

Should you wish to purchase your own rifle, then a Firearm Certificate is necessary. This is obtained from the Chief Officer of Police of the area in which you live, and an application form can be obtained from any police station. The questions on the application form are quite straightforward, mainly concerning the use for which the weapon is to be put, where it is to be used, the amount of

A knobber – a young stag. Beasts which stray on to agricultural land may be shot throughout the year, but this is not stalking.

173

ammunition which the applicant wishes to purchase and the applicant's character. The application has to be endorsed by someone other than a member of the family who knows the applicant personally – a doctor, police officer, minister or Justice of the Peace will do nicely. The Chief of Police will grant a certificate, provided he is satisfied that the applicant has a good reason for obtaining the weapon and that there is no danger to public safety or the peace.

That is the theory. In practice, some police areas grant certificates more readily than others, and the ease with which you obtain your certificate will depend largely on where you happen to live. Special arrangements can be made for sportsmen visiting the United Kingdom. They should apply well in advance to the police in the area where they will be residing, and either a certificate or a temporary permit can be issued, subject to the police being satisfied that the normal conditions are met.

VENISON SALES

One final piece of legislation which may be of interest to the stalker is that concerned with the sale of venison. Under the provisions of the Deer (Scotland) Act, 1959 it is an offence to sell, possess, or transport venison for the purpose of sale unless you are a licensed dealer, in possession or transporting the venison for the purpose of selling to a licensed dealer, or you have purchased the venison from a licensed dealer. It would appear from this that, if you buy a carcase from the estate where you have been stalking, and intend to sell part of it to friends rather than keep the whole thing for yourself, then, strictly speaking, you are committing an offence.

This is, of necessity, only a brief resumé of the law relating to deer stalking and firearms. If you wish to read further, then I would recommend *Fair Game* by Charlie Parkes and John Thornley (Pelham Books, 1987) which looks at all the law relating to field sports in considerable detail.

13

Obtaining Stalking

For many people, particularly those resident south of the border, or overseas, Highland deer stalking must seem like an unattainable dream. Woodland stalking is available, but the killing of deer (red, roe, sika or fallow), in the woods and forests is a totally different sport from the pursuit of the red deer of the Highlands. I do not mean to belittle the sport of woodland stalking – it is a highly skilled and demanding field sport – but it is not deer stalking in the sense of the sport which is carried out in the hills of Scotland.

With the various species of deer being widespread throughout England and Wales there are plenty of opportunities for the keen stalker to lease stalking rights, often within easy reach of his home. There are hotels, forestry owners and sporting estates which let out stalking by the day or by the season, and in some cases, where marauding deer create problems, farmers may be glad to obtain the services of a competent stalker.

Highland stalking is a different matter. For a start the majority of would-be stalkers probably live a long way from the deer of the Highlands. There is no chance of nipping out for a couple of hours' stalking before work, or dropping in to the woods as the dusk falls on a summer's evening. A trip to the Highlands means careful planning, a long journey, a week's holiday devoted to stalking and considerable expense. Perhaps the hardest part for the novice is knowing where to begin in attempting to arrange a stalking trip.

Red deer have a range of something over 7¾ million acres in Scotland. Most, but not all, of this comprises the deer forests where stags and hinds are encouraged to live and are stalked for sport. By the nature of the sport, most deer forests are large areas of wild, undeveloped land, and the ownership of that land lies, generally, with those wealthy enough to preserve such areas primarily for sport. It is most unusual for the sporting rights on a deer forest to be let out for a period of years as is often the case with stalking rights in woodland blocks in the south. Instead, the owner will let out short periods of a week to a month, reserving the rest of the season for himself or his guests.

Since the season for stag stalking lasts for something over three months, followed by four months hind stalking, very few owners are able, or would wish, to spend the whole season on their estates. It is, therefore, common to let out the stalking during those times that the owner does not wish to retain it for himself, and it is this that provides the chance for the novice to take up the sport.

The problem for the newcomer to stalking is knowing where to go and who to approach in order to arrange a stalking foray. Does he make a direct approach to the landowner, contact the owner's agent or factor, book a stalking holiday

A fine stag still in velvet in mid-July. Stalking for trophy beasts such as this may well be more expensive than simply culling the rubbish.

through a hotel, use the services of a sporting agency, or try to join a party which is being formed by someone with a short lease already arranged? In fact, all of these are realistic possibilities, and the method to be recommended will depend on the individual circumstances of the would-be stalker.

A direct approach to landowner or agent may be successful, but does presuppose that you know not only which estates have free dates in their stalking calendar but also the right person to contact for those estates. Many owners and factors will be suspicious of an approach from someone totally unknown to them, but this does not rule out the possibility of picking up some stalking in this way. You might be lucky with your first letter or telephone call. Equally, you may spend a lot on postage or calls to no effect. If you already know someone who has stalking to let, or have a friend who does, and will provide a reference for you, then things should be much simpler.

Many hotels advertise stalking holidays for their customers. If you want to try a stalking break based in hotel accommodation, then the classified advertisements in the *Shooting Times*, *Field* and similar magazines will offer you a choice of venues. Obviously, it is vital to make sure that the hotel understands that you want to stalk during your stay before you arrive on their doorstep. They may have to make prior arrangements with a local estate and in any case the number of guests who can stalk on any one day will obviously be limited.

Hotel stalking can be an excellent way of sampling the sport, but for many experienced stalkers the pleasure of a stalking holiday lies not just in the time spent on the hill, but in the whole, often rather antiquated, atmosphere of life in

October on the hill, and this stag answers a roar from the stalker. Stalking during the rut is very popular.

a stalking lodge. If this is the way in which you choose to pursue your Highland stalking then some form of estate lease is what is required. Assuming that you do not have the contacts to make a direct approach to a stalking estate, then the simplest way to arrange your stalking is almost certainly to use the services of a sporting agent.

Traditionally, sporting agents have played a very important role in the letting of stalking and other sporting activities in the Highlands. One of the early and more successful agencies was established by Tom Speedy around the turn of the century, and since then the majority of sporting lets have been handled by agents. Many, perhaps most, estate owners have too little time to concern themselves with the minutiae of arranging sporting lets, so it is natural that this task should be delegated. In some cases, the factor may deal with sporting lets, but even those estates which have their own factors, or are factored by one of the large estate management companies, may still let their stalking through an agent.

Many of the professional firms of estate agents will have their own specialist sporting agency, of course. With many of the deer forests being owned by absentee landlords the use of an agent to let out property has long been an established source of extra revenue. It is estimated that as many as 80 per cent of the annual stalking lets in the Highlands are handled by agencies or individual agents.

A good agent, and it is obviously important that the agent is both reputable and capable, will work to the advantage of both owner and tenant. In case that sounds like a contradiction let me explain further. The owner wants revenue from his estate, but not at the expense of his peace of mind. He therefore hopes for a 'civilised' tenant who will not damage his property, his reputation or his sporting prospects by over-shooting. The tenant looks for good sport, value for money and continuity. The agent, who receives a commission from both parties, must try to ensure that both owner and tenant are satisfied with the arrangement. The owner must be satisfied that his estate has been properly cared for by its temporary custodian, and the tenant should be satisfied that he has received good value for his outlay. Then both will probably make use of the agent again in the following seasons.

It is normal for stalking during the stag shooting season to be let by the week, the fee charged to include a specified number of stags, lodge accommodation if this is available and any other sport, such as a grouse shooting, trout or salmon fishing, which may be offered. At one time many estates were let out on long-term leases, but this is virtually unknown today, on either a long- or short-term basis, unless the prospective tenant is known to the owner or his land agent. The demand for short-term stalking lets, and the rapid increase in prices, mean that any spare dates in the calendar can be easily and profitably filled without entering into long-term commitments.

There are occasions when lets of one, two or three days may be available – attractive to someone who wants to sample a day on the hill without actually committing themselves to a full week's stalking. These are most likely to occur where there is no lodge accommodation available with the stalking; where the

Other sport available will affect the cost of a let. Here a guest uses a big, double-handed rod for salmon.

estate is too small to be able to provide a full week's sport, or perhaps early in the season on a hind forest before the stags break out. Sometimes odd days may become available at short notice where some problem has left a gap in the programme. This could be to fill in a broken week or to catch up on numbers where bad weather has meant that insufficient stags have been shot and the end of the season is near.

A number of factors will control the price of a sporting let. Obviously, the greater the demand, the higher the fee that can, and almost certainly will, be charged. Among the factors that will increase the demand and therefore the saleability of a forest are the following.

1   How well known the forest is. A 'name' forest will command a higher price than an unknown one.
2   The size and quality of the stags on the forest. A forest that produces trophy heads and above average body weights will be more attractive than one with less mature stags in the cull.
3   The number of beats that can be stalked each day. If two, or perhaps three Rifles can be sent to the hill each day then the attraction, and price, of the let will rise accordingly.
4   The time of year. Stalking during the rut (late September to the end of the season), is much sought after, and priced acccordingly.
5   The manner in which the stalking is organised. The provision of the traditional accoutrements such as ghillies and ponies adds to the desirability of a stalking let.
6   The existence of other sport. If there is dogging for grouse, trout and salmon fishing or perhaps some woodland stalking for roe or sika, this will also increase the price.

The more of these features that an estate has, the more in demand will it be for sporting lets and the price will naturally reflect that demand. It is a general rule that once a tenancy has been satisfactorily established, then that tenant holds an unwritten right to have first chance of that week in subsequent years. This is not a legal right, just the way in which things are done. Tenants will often hold on to 'their' week for grim death, particularly since rents tend to remain steady for existing tenants but rise sharply when a new let is organised. If you have a good week and lose it, a replacement, if one can be found, may prove to be much more expensive.

Hind stalking is let by the day as well as by the week, and is often arranged without accommodation. The usual time for letting hind stalking is in late November and early December, even though the season continues until mid-February. This is partly due to the uncertainty of the weather at the beginning of the year, but also because many estates would hope to complete the bulk of their cull during the first part of the season.

While hind stalking is still not too difficult to find it is possible that there has been a reduction in the number of forests letting out hind stalking in recent years. As the trend towards more scientific deer management makes the hind

Many forests will carry a stock of grouse, and dogging over pointers or setters may be available as well as stalking.

cull much more selective than was once the case, many owners prefer their stalkers to carry out the shooting themselves. The days when a Rifle might be advised to shoot 'wherever they're thickest and blackest', i.e. shoot indiscriminately into a bunch of hinds hoping to kill several with one shot, are, hopefully long past. In general, hind stalking should be cheaper than stag stalking and, if you are lucky with the weather, can be quite marvellous sport. Of course, if you are unlucky with Highland winter weather then there may be no sport at all.

Magazines such as the *Shooting Times*, the *Field* and *Country Life* will carry advertisements from sporting agencies, particularly if you purchase one of the special issues such as the 'Stalking' or 'Sport in Scotland' numbers which the *Shooting Times* produces from time to time. The more information that you can provide an agent with, the more likely he is to be able to help you find the kind of stalking that you are looking for. Will you be planning your holiday alone, with your wife or husband or with a party of friends? Do you want just stalking, or a variety of other sporting activities? When do you want to go, what previous experience have you had, how fit will the members of the party be? How large is your budget? Are you planning to self-cater, or will you want meals cooked for you? The list is almost inexhaustible.

A good agent will do his best to find a tenancy that will suit your requirements. It may be that you can be fitted in with another party; it is not necessary for an individual to undertake the let on his own. There are obvious attractions in making up a party from among a group of friends, but if you do not have enough acquaintances with an interest in stalking, then it is likely that you can be matched in with a group which has spare capacity.

Hind stalking may be easier to obtain, and cheaper, than stalking stags, but conditions can be very harsh.

The sporting magazines also carry advertisements from some deer forests which have vacancies for stalking. Obviously a direct approach to one of these advertisers will meet with a warmer reception than cold canvassing is likely to achieve. I have occasionally seen advertisements for the organisers of a party who have taken a let but still require some extra people to complete their numbers, though such advertisements are quite rare. There is, of course, nothing to prevent the would-be stalker from placing his own advertisement stating the time and type of sport that he is seeking.

The first trip to the Highlands is probably the most difficult to arrange, unless you are invited as a guest to a stalking estate. Once you have been, sampled the sport, made one or two contacts such as the stalker and factor, and shown yourself to be safe and competent, then future trips should be easier to organise. The stalkers' grapevine will often have the earliest knowledge of which tenancies are not being renewed the following season, and such information can be invaluable if you are looking for stalking. Many of the best tenancies are never advertised at all, being transferred 'on recommendation'.

The price of a stalking holiday is constantly changing, so I will not attempt to indicate the likely cost. Any figures that I did give would be quickly outdated. However, it can be very favourably priced when compared with other activitiy holidays. The amount you will have to pay will depend, largely, on the peripheral parts of the package – the standard of accommodation, food and drink, the other sport included in the let, the reputation of the forest and its accessibility, the time of the year when you go and whether you want to stalk stags or hinds. The most expensive package is not necessarily the best, particularly where the quality of the actual stalking is concerned.

14

Stalking Organisations

Every sport has its clubs and societies and deer stalking is no exception. There are two main organisations concerned with deer in Britain – The British Deer Society and The St Hubert Club of Great Britain, plus a Government body, the Red Deer Commission, and the British Field Sports Society which has a general, but less specific, interest in deer. Each fulfils a very different role in their dealings with the red deer and a case can be made for the stalker to be a member of all three which are open to him or her. As a statutory body, The Red Deer Commission is obviously not open to membership by the general public.

THE BRITISH DEER SOCIETY

The British Deer Society (BDS) is a charity, formed in 1963 and devoted solely to the welfare of deer. It is not simply a society for stalkers, indeed, members are specifically forbidden to use their membership of the Society as a means of obtaining stalking. Everyone with an interest in deer is welcomed by the Society, be they stalker, photographer, farmer, forester, naturalist or just someone who likes deer. The Society produces an excellent magazine, *Deer*, which is sent to members three times a year in March, July and November and contains photographs, articles and editorials on a wide variety of deer related topics.

The Society has an information service which will advise members on any subject connected with deer, including biology, photography, stalking, management and the law. There is an education programme of general interest plus more specific courses which are run on woodland stalking, highland stalking and deer management.

The Society supports certain research projects which are of benefit to deer and publishes the results of research from other sources. There are a number of branches throughout Britain and Ireland, and each branch will organise activities and meetings for its members. There are photographic and rifle shooting competitions, visits to deer farms, forests and parks, film and slide shows, lectures, discussions and various fund raising activities. Free insurance for public liability while stalking is provided for members.

As a charity, the Society is forbidden to take part in political lobbying, but this does not prevent the giving of advice on problems and legislation pertaining to deer, firearms used for stalking, poaching and deer protection. The Society has been consulted by the Home Office in relation to proposed new legislation on

A stag down among the trees in spring, antlers just starting to re-grow.

Stags can be quite aggressive, even to their own hinds, during the rut.

firearms control and is involved in advising on topics which concern deer in draft reports from the European Commission to FACE (Federation of Field Sports Associations of the EEC). The BDS Chairman, Hugh Oliver-Bellais, considers the work with FACE to be a vital part of the BDS work since, without the restraining influence of the Association, some EEC legislation could be very damaging to sportsmen.

In addition to their work with FACE, the BDS is involved in discussions with many internal bodies, including the Nature Conservancy Council, the Forestry Commission, the Ministry of Agriculture and the Department of the Environment. Much of the good work carried out by the Society, and by its officers, will go unnoticed by stalkers, but in providing expert and realistic advice to many bodies which have the power to affect the deer population but very little real knowledge, there can be no doubt that the Society provides a very real service to stalkers and all others who have the welfare of our native deer at heart.

The aims of the Society, as stated in their pamphlet *What is the British Deer Society?* are: the study and dissemination of knowledge of deer, the promotion of proper and humane methods of deer management and the provision of advice on all matters relating to deer. Such aims should find a sympathetic reception from any deer stalker.

Membership of the Society costs £12.50 per year in Britain, £15.00 per year in Europe and £17.00 per year elsewhere. There are special rates available to children, professional stalkers and forestry workers, and corporate bodies. The magazine alone is probably worth the membership fee, and I would highly recommend membership to anyone with more than a passing interest in deer. The address is:

> The Membership Secretary
> The British Deer Society
> Church Farm
> Lower Basildon
> Reading
> Berkshire RG8 9NH

THE ST HUBERT CLUB OF GREAT BRITAIN

The St Hubert Club of Great Britain is a private club with membership currently limited to 350 individuals. A prospective member must be proposed and seconded, then vetted by the club before being admitted, unlike the BDS where membership is open to everyone.

The St Hubert Club is principally concerned with stalking – mainly low-ground rather than Highland stalking – and it is the main organisation in Britain concerned with stalking as a sport rather than with deer in general. There is an excellent, and very well structured system of education and training for members, with instruction and testing in deer recognition, range firing, safety, field shooting, fieldcraft and use of high seats. It takes about four years for a novice to complete the full range of training, and the club undoubtedly provides the fullest educational and training programme available to the non-professional stalker.

The club does cull work for the Forestry Commission, and offers a culling service to other landowners who may have a deer problem. They exhibit annually at the Game Fair, and hold a yearly exhibition of the heads, trophy and otherwise, taken by members during the season. The better heads will be judged to see which are of bronze, silver or gold medal standard according to the CIC Formula (Conseil International de la Chasse).

Further details of the St Hubert Club of Great Britain may be obtained from the Secretary:

> Mr Peter E. Whitaker
> Boundary House
> Halton Village
> Aylesbury
> Buckinghamshire HP22 5PD

Aggression is not confined to the stags. This hind determinedly chased the knobber out, striking at him repeatedly with a forefoot.

THE BRITISH FIELD SPORTS SOCIETY

As a registered charity, the British Deer Society is forbidden to engage in political activity. In contrast, it is probably fair to say that the primary work of the British Field Sports Society (BFSS) involves lobbying through its Parliamentary Committee to ensure the future of all field sports in Great Britain. While deer stalking is not one of the primary targets of the various anti-field sports organisations, it is probably true to say that, should the antis succeed in outlawing hunting and shooting, their attentions would turn to the remaining field sports. There are already some ominous noises being made about fishing, probably more muted than might otherwise be the case because of the sheer number of anglers, most of whom are also voters. Though stalking is generally free of the attentions of the anti lobby at the moment, it is unlikely to remain that way for ever, and the BFSS has the political muscle and experience that will be needed when that day comes.

The BFSS runs a stalking course on the Isle of Rhum every year, administered by the Society's Advisory Committee on Stalking. There are Advisory Committees for Fishing, Hunting, Shooting, Hare Coursing and Falconry as well as the one concerned with stalking, and the Society has representatives on, or contact with, many other bodies as diverse as the National Anglers' Council, the Captive Hawk Board, The Game Conservancy and the British Association for Shooting and Conservation.

The BFSS has a specialist political staff which maintains contact with relevant Ministries and a Parliamentary Committee which opposes any legislation which would ban or needlessly curtail traditional field sports in Britain. The Society undertakes to keep the public informed of the true nature of field sports by distributing material to the media, lecturing in schools and to clubs, attending country shows and publishing books and leaflets. They work for the preservation of habitat, the curtailing of harmful chemicals, the prevention of pollution and the prosecution of poachers. Their work helps to safeguard our traditional country pastimes from the attention of those who, through malice, or more often through ignorance, would seek to see them banned. The threat is real, and without the efforts of the British Field Sports Society, and bodies like them, many of our sports might already be no more than a memory from the past.

Membership of the Society is not expensive: £10 per year for an individual member, £18 per year for husband and wife and £25 per year for a family, with special rates for Life Members, Trade Members and Students. It may, one day, prove to be the best investment in your chosen sport that you have ever made. The address of the Society is:

British Field Sports Society
59 Kennington Road
London SE1 7PZ

A calf, just a few days old. All true stalkers have the welfare of the deer very much at heart.

THE RED DEER COMMISSION

The Red Deer Commission differs from the other organisations in that it is a government body, not a club or society open to membership by the public. The Commission was set up by Parliament in 1959, with the responsibility of furthering the conservation and control of red deer in Scotland. The Deer (Amendment) (Scotland) Act, 1982 gave the Commission responsibility for sika, sika/red crosses and to some extent roe and fallow in addition to red deer. The members of the Commission are appointed by the Secretary of State for Scotland from nominees of the Nature Conservancy Council, the Natural Environment Research Council, members representing landowning and sporting interests and others representing farming and crofting interests.

The RDC has a broad remit to consider all aspects of deer management and control. There are many areas of conflict between the owners and occupiers of land where deer are concerned, particularly between the owners of stalking forests and the farming and crofting interests which border them. The RDC advises the Forestry Commission, private forestry companies and individuals about grant schemes and forestry protection and offers advice and practical assistance in cases of deer damage. In addition, the RDC advises the Secretary of State on all matters related to deer.

The Commission undertakes control work where it is considered necessary, though the person legally entitled to cull the deer would always be consulted before the Commission's stalkers would take action. They carry out census work on the deer population, mark calves for future study, advise estates on their deer management policies and assist in the setting up of co-operative management schemes between neighbouring estates.

The Commission publishes a number of booklets and pamphlets of interest to deer managers and stalkers and most of these are available, free of charge, from the Commission's offices in Inverness. Their *Code of Practice for Shooting Deer* is an excellent little booklet which every stalker should have on his bookshelf, and the wall chart showing how to carry out larder work is clear and easy to follow.

Many estates take a jaw from every beast shot and send it to the RDC for ageing. This is a valuable service to the estate, monitoring how well they are carrying out their annual cull, as well as providing much needed raw data for the Commission's own researches. The headquarters of The Red Deer Commission is in Inverness. The address is:

The Red Deer Commission
Knowsley
82 Fairfield Road
Inverness

Bibliography

Ackroyd, Charles H., *A Veteran Sportsman's Diary* (R. Carruthers and Sons, 1926)

Clutton-Brock, T. H., Guiness, F. E., and Albon, S. D., *Red Deer – Behaviour and Ecology of Two Sexes* (Edinburgh University Press, 1982)

Grant, Matt and Bruce, *The Sharp Shooter* (A. H. and A. W. Reed Ltd., 1972)

Hart-Davis, Duff, *Monarchs of the Glen* (Jonathon Cape, 1978)

Parkes, Charlie, and Thornley, John, *Fair Game* (Pelham Books, 1987)

Scrope, William, *The Art of Deer-Stalking* (Edward Arnold, 1838)

  Red Deer Management (The Red Deer Commission, 1981)

The Marchioness of Londonderry, *Henry Chaplin: A Memoir* (Macmillan, 1926)

Index